A COLLECTOR'S RECOLLECTIONS
GEORGE ARTHUR PLIMPTON

Edited by

Pauline Ames Plimpton

With a Foreword by

George Plimpton

Published by the Columbia University Libraries
New York   1993

Z473
.P56
A3
1993

Published by the Columbia University Libraries and produced by the Columbia University Office of Publications.

Printed in the United States of America.

PRODUCTION EDITOR: Debra Helfand

DESIGNER: Doreen Pastore

ISBN 0-9607862-6-0

For his Namesake,
George A. Plimpton

And we shall speak of thee some-
what, I trowe,
when thou art gone

Chaucer

ALSO BY PAULINE AMES PLIMPTON

Ramblings about Borderland (1974)

Orchids at Christmas (1975)

Ancestry of Blanche Butler Ames and Adelbert Ames (1977)

Oakes Ames—Jottings of a Harvard Botanist (1979)

The Plimpton Papers—Law and Diplomacy (1985)

A Window on Our World (1989)

Butler Ames and the Villa Balbianello (1991)

TABLE OF CONTENTS

ILLUSTRATIONS

George Arthur Plimpton, 1855–1936

PREFACE

When Pauline Ames Plimpton suggested that the Columbia University Libraries publish the memoirs of her late father-in-law, George Arthur Plimpton (1855–1936), I knew that this was a project that deserved our consideration, given Mr. Plimpton's close association with the Libraries in the '20s and '30s. What I could not know, of course, until I had read the manuscript, were the other Columbia associations that appear throughout. George Arthur Plimpton, for instance, singles out for special praise a course taught at Amherst by John W. Burgess on the development of constitutional government. Burgess would later come to Columbia and leave his collection to the Libraries, where it forms part of the Burgess-Carpenter Library, a collection used today by Columbia's undergraduates. And it was Melvil Dewey, Columbia's librarian in the 1880s, who pledged Plimpton to his fraternity at Amherst and who made his introductions to the publishing business, a providential meeting for Plimpton, publishing, and, ultimately, Columbia's Libraries.

Later, when he was the head of Ginn & Company in New York, George Arthur Plimpton hosted the luncheon at which the Friends of the Columbia University Libraries was founded and went on to serve as its first chairman from 1928 until his death. In 1935–1936, he generously gave to Columbia's Rare Book and Manuscript Library a seminal collection of rare volumes and medieval and Renaissance manuscripts. The memoirs explain how he found some of the more important items in his collection, items that, to this day, attract scholars from throughout the country to the Rare Book and Manuscript Library. Also included with these memoirs is a set of delightful letters from George Arthur Plimpton to his son, Francis T. P. Plimpton (1900–1983). Francis Plimpton grew up to marry Pauline Ames; he also served as deputy United States representative to the United Nations (1961–1965), represented New York City as its official greeter, and founded one of Manhattan's largest and most prestigious law firms, Debevoise & Plimpton. Somehow he managed to find the

1

time to be a founding member of Columbia's "reconstituted" Friends of the Libraries in 1951 (the original group faded away shortly after the elder Plimpton's death) and to serve as its vice chairman in the 1960s. (His brother, Calvin Hastings Plimpton, a retired physician and former president of Amherst College, remains a Friend to this day.)

Pauline Ames Plimpton, who for years has been a member of the Council of the Friends of the Libraries, has lovingly collected and edited these memoirs, written the introduction, and elicited a foreword from her son George. Clearly, the Columbia University Libraries owes a debt of gratitude to the Plimpton family, whose friendship has helped to sustain it for more than six decades. With this volume, the Libraries celebrates that friendship and commemorates this family's strong and loyal support.

ELAINE SLOAN
**Vice President for Information Services
and University Librarian
April 2, 1993**

FOREWORD

My childhood memories of my grandfather are regrettably few. He died when I was nine. I have an image of a somewhat stout gentleman in heavy, shapeless suits, which I now know he had made up locally in Walpole from sheep he raised at the Lewis Farm. I must have been taken to the funeral. I read now from the obituaries that no less than five reverends conducted the services in Walpole, and that among the honorary pallbearers were university presidents, educa-

The Lewis Farm from East Street after the Barn was remodeled, 1933

tors, library directors, publishers, and a justice of the U.S. Supreme Court (Harlan F. Stone). On that day my father wore a black band on his sleeve as a sign of mourning and he kept it there for a year—very much the custom then, though no longer. How odd! Only athletic teams wear black bands on their uniforms to indicate mourning for someone closely associated with the organization.

I would suppose sitting there in the church that day the congregation spent much of its time reflecting on the life of the extraordinary man it had come to honor. I, uncomfortable sitting in the wooden pews, and doubtless squirming, must have done the same in a more limited way. Most likely I replayed in my mind's eye a scene I can remember with great clarity to this day—a Christmas afternoon we were taken to spend with him at his home at 61 Park Avenue in New York City's Murray Bay section when I was probably five or six years old. I was motioned over to where he was sitting in an armchair. He took out a large pocket-watch from his waistcoat; dangling it briefly from a long, gold-linked chain, and holding it in the palm of his hand, then announced that he was going to perform an act of magic. He held up the watch and asked me to blow on its closed lid. I did so. Nothing happened.

"Blow harder!"

I did, and to my surprise the cover of the watch sprang open, indeed as if by magic.

He then showed us (my younger brother was standing alongside) how the "magic" worked—a little button on the rim of the watch that, when pushed, popped open the case.

I recall at this point that "Santa Claus" emerged from the vicinity of the fireplace—an illusion also explained, in this case by the fact that his white beard slipped down and revealed my uncle Calvin.

So, sitting in the church, I must have remembered that afternoon. And certainly I must have recalled times at the Lewis Farm, inspecting those aforementioned sheep, and so on, though what I particularly remember was a wing to the Farm called "The Barn," which looked more like a theater (there was a small stage at one end for amateur theatrics) though in fact it was a converted cowbarn. On its white-painted walls was a remarkable collection of early Americana— broadsheets, flyers, proclamations, slave auction announcements, calls to arms—that in sum offered a kind of diorama of the early history of New England. There was a badminton court in the center of the Barn—on which my grandfather played into his seventies, albeit from a "somewhat stationary position" as my father once described it—but while I played the game or tried to, what I particularly remember were those walls, my imagination soaring as I laboriously studied the framed evidence of those momentous times. In a sense, the Barn typified my grandfather's absorption with the past, collecting artifacts so that events could be conjured up far more vividly than they could be gained from history books.

Fanny Hastings (Ann) Plimpton sitting in the remodeled Barn, which housed the collections and a badminton court

I don't remember the more scholarly things he collected—the hornbooks, the Greek manuscripts, the early medieval tracts, the samplers, the antiphonals, early maps, fifteenth-century arithmetic books, thirteenth-century grammars—hardly the sort of fare my grandfather could interest me in; a tour of the Barn was about all I could handle at that age.

The only items that might have been of interest to my young eyes would have been his wooden cigar store Indians. These he collected by approaching guileless cigar store proprietors and offering to remove the wooden Indians from in front of their stores *without charge.* The courtyard at the Lewis Farm contained this collection—a somewhat imposing group considering the stern visages the sculptors carved on the Indians' heads.

Perhaps my grandfather showed me one of his beloved hornbooks—his collection of twenty-four was the largest in the world; his fellow-collector, J. P. Morgan, had only one—letting me hold the hand-mirror-like artifact by the handle

The remodeled Barn

and telling me that this schoolboy object was how I would have learned my ABCs and my numbers if I were Shakespeare or Chaucer, undoubtedly having to explain to me as we went along who these two worthies were.

Perhaps (yet another "perhaps"!) he found time to tell me about an organization he belonged to called The Hobby Club—a group of collectors who had dinners at which they featured their prized possessions. One of them collected armor. Someone told me (probably Father, but perhaps Grandfather), and it has stayed with me over the years, that the guests *wore* the armor at this particular occasion, clanking

in to have supper. My grandfather, as well as the others, must
have been hard-pressed to match *that* evening!

One of the institutions in which my grandfather had an
abiding interest was the Folger Shakespeare Library in Washington, D.C. Its founder, Henry Clay Folger, and my grandfather had curiously parallel careers as collectors.   Both were

Little Princess Pocahontas and Chief Negaset, two figures from George Arthur
Plimpton's collection of wooden cigar store Indians

students at Amherst, both came from families of relatively
limited means, both were ignited very early to follow careers
as collectors. Folger's epiphany came at Amherst when he
paid twenty-five cents to hear a lecture by Ralph Waldo
Emerson. From that point on, he began a collection that

eventually became the largest gathering of Shakespeariana ever assembled anywhere.

My grandfather differed from Folger, though, in that his interest turned out to be far more eclectic. While Folger concentrated solely on Shakespeare, my grandfather spread his net wide . . . the entire field of learning. Folger undoubtedly had my grandfather's little book, *The Education of Shakespeare,* but probably not my grandfather's second volume on the education of Chaucer.

Part of a small and lovely collection is included in the present volume—having not to do with the education of either Shakespeare or Chaucer but my father! These are a few examples of the letters my grandfather wrote Father to let him know some of the wonders that awaited him when he finished school and got out into the world. In a way they are extensions of his hornbooks—rather more elaborate, obviously, with the pasted-in photographs and postcards, always not only personal but instructive.

My grandfather probably thought that the most important legacy he could pass on were his collections and their great value to future generations of students and scholars. How opportune that this volume has now been added to the whole . . .

GEORGE AMES PLIMPTON

INTRODUCTION

George Arthur Plimpton (1855–1936) was the senior partner of Ginn & Company, New York publishers of educational textbooks, and a famous bibliophile. He had the rare good fortune to combine his vocation with his avocation, for he collected rare textbooks and medieval manuscripts pertaining to education. Eventually, he owned the largest collection of educational works in the world.

He was born in Walpole, Massachusetts, in a house with four Doric columns known as the Homestead. He was descended from a Sergeant John Plympton of Deerfield, Massachusetts, who was captured by the Indians during the French and Indian Wars and was burned at the stake.

Although as a publisher George Arthur Plimpton spent much of his time in New York City, he was devoted to his Walpole home, the Lewis Farm. During his lifetime, he donated to his native town a forest, sites for several schools, and a fountain in memory of the townsmen who had served in the French and Indian Wars. In Walpole he built up a large dairy, ground his own flour, and raised sheep for wool. He proudly wore suits made from cloth woven by the women in the village. He liked to tell the story about the time he sat beside a man on the Knickerbocker Limited to New York and boasted about owning twenty-four blackfaced highland sheep, and the man turned out to be a Scotchman who owned fourteen *thousand* blackfaced sheep.

In 1892 he married Frances Taylor Pearsons, a descendant of Edward Taylor of Westfield, one of the earliest American poets. She was a daughter of the mayor of Holyoke and a niece of Judge W. B. C. Pearsons, a benefactor of Mount Holyoke and other small liberal arts colleges across the country. She died in 1900 at the birth of their son—my husband—Francis Taylor Pearsons Plimpton.

George Arthur Plimpton was married again in 1917, to Fanny Hastings of New York and Bermuda, daughter of General Russell Hastings (who developed the farming of onions and Easter lilies on Bermuda), and a grandniece of

Frances Taylor Pearsons Plimpton, first wife of George Arthur Plimpton

President Rutherford B. Hayes. She worked for Serbian Relief during World War I, and after their marriage she took courses at Columbia so she could help her husband with his collections and books. They had a son, Calvin Hastings, and a daughter, Emily.

Unlike many collectors, George Arthur Plimpton loved to handle and display his treasures, which were kept at hand in a vault under his town house at 61 Park Avenue. He often invited groups of friends, Century Association members, or school teachers home for the evening. He would bring up from the vault his manuscripts, horn books, or early arithmetics to talk about them and their history, and he would show them off with the greatest delight. He invariably finished the evening with ice cream and after-dinner coffee. He was even willing to carry parts of his valuable collection in a cardboard suitcase when he traveled to speak at colleges and universities throughout the country or at Oxford and Cambridge.

Based on the manuscripts and first editions in his library, George Arthur Plimpton wrote two books, *The Education of Shakespeare* and *The Education of Chaucer*. In the preface to *The Education of Shakespeare,* he says of his collection: "I had the privilege to get together the manuscripts and books which are more or less responsible for our present civilization because they are the books from which the youth of many centuries have received their education."

He was a great friend and close associate of Professor David Eugene Smith of Columbia University. Professor Smith was the author of *Rara Arithmetica,* a book based on the Plimpton collection. Together they were the founders of the Friends of the Columbia Libraries. In 1935—the year before his death—George Arthur Plimpton donated his collection to the Rare Book and Manuscript Library of Columbia, a collection containing twenty thousand manuscripts and early editions of what he called "our tools of learning" or "the Tower of Knowledge."

George Arthur Plimpton was an avid collector of all sorts of things. In memory of his first wife, Frances Taylor Pearsons Plimpton, he presented to Wellesley College, her alma mater (class of 1884), a library of rare Italian books and manuscripts chiefly of the fourteenth and fifteenth centuries. Wellesley's rare book library is now said to have more Plutarchs than any other library in the country.

He had a famous collection of samplers, some sewn by his own ancestors; a unique collection of wooden cigar store Indians, now virtually unattainable; and a collection of antiphonals and illuminated manuscripts. He also put together a collection of contemporary portraits of English authors unequalled even by the National Portrait Gallery in London. These paintings hung on the walls of the President's House at Amherst College during the administration (1960–1971) of his second son, Dr. Calvin Hastings Plimpton. The portraits still belong to Dr. Plimpton.

There seemed to be no end to the variety of what interested him. He bought the oak paneling from Lord North's house in London when it was torn down; he salvaged the brick fireplace from Sir Isaac Newton's house, which had also been the home of Fanny Burney. These decorate the library of his Amherst fraternity house, Delta Kappa Epsilon, which was refurbished as a dormitory after the abolishment of the fraternity system and is now called Plimpton House.

Two antiphonals from George Arthur Plimpton's collection

When he traveled to the Far East in 1920 for Ginn & Company, he stayed at the Canton Christian College (Lingnan University) in South China and bought land containing some Chinese ancestral graves. He donated this land to the university, giving it room to expand. In Japan he presented a girls' dormitory to Doshisha University, which was founded by a Japanese contemporary of his at Amherst College.

His private papers are full of letters to important men of the time, including Andrew Carnegie, J. P. Morgan, John D. Rockefeller, and Henry Clay Folger.

There are two stories I like about George Arthur Plimpton as a collector. According to the first, one day on a street corner he met Mr. Folger, the founder of the Folger Shakespeare Library in Washington, D.C. The two elderly gentlemen began comparing notes on their collections. Mr. Plimpton revealed that he had just written overseas, special delivery, for Queen Elizabeth's corsets, which had come on the market. Mr. Folger replied, "I've got them, I *cabled!*" (Actually, the Folger Library may have them, but their authenticity is now considered questionable!) Despite their rivalry, Mr. Plimpton was a trustee of the Library. On one occasion Mrs. Folger presented him with the key of the Folger Shakespeare Library, using a phrase of Shakespeare's: "I would you accept of grace and love this key to our hearts."

The second story concerns seven vellum leaves of a Coptic manuscript of the late ninth century. They were a gift from one of his partners, who found them on a trip up the Nile. It was discovered that they were the missing leaves of the Morgan Library Coptic manuscript 594. Mr. Plimpton suggested to the elder Morgan that all the leaves should be brought together, and suggested that he could not properly part with his own leaves, as they had been a gift; Mr. Morgan did not take the hint, and the two sets of leaves are still held separately.

George Arthur Plimpton was, moreover, a collector of trusteeships—Amherst, Exeter, Barnard, Union Theological Seminary, Constantinople College for Women (now part of Robert's College). Amherst was his alma mater (class of 1876), and he served as president of the board for thirty-five years. He was also a benefactor to many of these institutions. To Amherst, for instance, he presented an interesting theatrical collection and an extensive collection relating to the French and Indian Wars—particularly to Lord Jeffrey Amherst—that comprises a wide variety of broadsides, contemporary maps, engravings, original letters, and other documents.

His school was Phillips Exeter Academy, from which he graduated in 1872. He was a trustee from 1903 to 1935 and served as chairman of the board for part of this time. His gifts to Exeter included the Plimpton Playing Fields and the Plimpton Playing Fields Beyond (a matchless expanse of some four hundred acres), the Phillips Church (the school church), and documents including the original 1638 deed of the town of Exeter from Indian Chief Wehanownowit to John Wheelwright. He also presented the school with a collection

George Arthur Plimpton and Calvin Coolidge, chairman of the Amherst Folger Committee, on the steps of the Folger Library on April 23, 1932. They are leaving the ceremony at which Mrs. Folger turned over the key of the Library to Mr. Plimpton, who, as president of the Amherst College Board of Trustees, accepted the gift for the College. On the platform were the Amherst trustees, presidents of half a dozen universities, the diplomatic corps, and other honored guests, including President Hoover.

relating to slavery in the pre-Civil War South, where he had traveled as a schoolbook salesman in his youth.

Always a benefactor, his enthusiasm persuaded others to be generous as well. I remember hearing the story of how he would stop in to see an old gentleman, Mr. Horace Walpole Carpentier, on his way home from his office. Mr. Carpentier had no relatives or close friends except for a collie dog, and when he died he left his entire estate of $1,500,000 to Barnard College.

Barnard College was a consuming interest for George Arthur Plimpton. A firm believer in education for women, he was one of those responsible for Barnard's founding. He became its treasurer in 1893, succeeding Jacob H. Schiff. He inherited two $1,000 bonds and $16,000 in debts. By the end of 1893 the college was free of debt, and he was instrumental in collecting enough money for the move to Morningside Heights. Despite the unpopularity at that time of the cause of higher education for women, he began "begging" with such success that, largely owing to his personal persuasive efforts, the college by the time of his death had nearly ten million dollars. Mr. Plimpton used to recall the day that the elder John D. Rockefeller took him aside, told how once long ago he had stood outside a church "begging" for money, and advised him, "Begging will do *you* good, too." Mr. Plimpton heeded the advice forthwith and successfully "begged" $250,000 from Mr. Rockefeller. On another occasion, Mr. Plimpton obtained $550,000 in a single gift from Jacob H. Schiff, Barnard's first treasurer. On his death, it was editorially suggested by the *New York Times* that a medal should be struck by Barnard College in honor of GEORGE A. PLIMPTON after the pattern of the old English coin called the "angel-noble," which would show him as St. Michael standing triumphantly over a dragon, for he had overcome one of the most menacing of modern dragons—a continuing college deficit.

For many years George Arthur Plimpton sat on the Board of Directors of the Constantinople College for Women. He was responsible for raising the funds that provided the college's impressive buildings overlooking the Bosphorus.

He was a trustee of the World Peace Foundation founded by his partner, Edwin Ginn, and a trustee and treasurer from the beginning of the Church Peace Union founded by Andrew Carnegie. The Church Peace Union has evolved into the Carnegie Council on Ethics and International Affairs. He also helped John W. Burgess form the Academy of Political Science and served as its treasurer; Ginn & Company published its *Political Science Quarterly.*

When he died, the *Columbia University Quarterly* said of him:

> ... in all these seemingly diverse activities there is a clear unity: his career was built on the inspiration of making the instruments and the opportunities of learning more rich, more accessible, and more stimulating. He bettered whatever he touched. His life was uncommonly rich and fruitful. He was born a comparatively poor boy, he died a great friend, patron, and exemplar of the high cause of learning, scholarship and enlightenment.

He has left some vivid recollections and remembrances, perhaps intending to write his autobiography. Some are diaries handwritten during voyages to England in the late 1880s; others were written in the 1920s and 1930s while he was on holiday. He demonstrates an amazing memory of his boyhood, education, and the beginnings of his career. His manuscript, written in such a straightforward, old-fashioned manner, catches the atmosphere of the past.

PAULINE AMES PLIMPTON

Autobiographical Writings of George Arthur Plimpton

Chapter I

My grandfather, Henry Plimpton, was born in Foxboro, Massachusetts, at a place called Crack Rock on January 28, 1787, one of three brothers and one sister.

At the age of sixteen, after the death of his father, he left the farm and became the first of his generation to enter into business, by going to Walpole and learning the iron business as an apprentice with Captain Josuah Stetson. He must have been very efficient, for on reaching his majority—that is, twenty-one years of age—he was taken into partnership and the firm became Stetson & Plimpton. They manufactured agricultural tools, among them hoes and things suitable for the farm. Associated with him as an apprentice was Oliver Ames.*

Subsequently, my grandfather withdrew from the firm and bought the right to dam the river at a place that afterwards became Plimptonville. He built his works there in 1816. Oliver Ames withdrew also and went to Bridgewater and there bought the water right to dam the river and built his works. Subsequently, an agreement was made that one should manufacture hoes and the other should manufacture shovels and they would not interfere with each other.

My grandfather built his house in 1816 near his works, previously having married Susanna Gay as his second wife on April 14, 1814. (His first wife was Sarah Fales, his cousin.

---

* Oliver Ames was my great-great-grandfather. He eventually bought the water privilege on the Queset River in North Easton, Massachusetts (a "privilege" carries the right to use a fall for motive power provided the owner does not interfere with the water supply of others). His works were called the Ames Shovel & Tool Company, and the O. Ames shovel became famous. His two sons, Oakes (my great-grandfather) and Oliver, financed and directed the building of the first transcontinental railroad, the Union Pacific. —Pauline Ames Plimpton

They had one daughter, Sally Plimpton.) He took young men with him to teach them the trade. These young men usually worked three years. They boarded with my grandfather and grandmother, and at the end of that time they were given fifty dollars and a suit of clothes.

My grandfather was interested in the only church in the town and was elected a deacon. That was the time when the church was controlled by the town and the ministers were elected by the town.

Along in 1826, after a bit of contest over the election of a minister to take the place of the Reverend Mr. Morey, who at that time was in his eightieth year, the question was whether they should have a Unitarian minister or follow in the lines of the orthodoxy. My grandfather was a strong upholder of orthodoxy and was against electing a minister of Unitarian faith. Finally, after the Unitarians succeeded in selecting the minister, my grandfather withdrew, and it is said that with six or seven women he established the orthodox church.

He was a man of great energy, enterprise, and strong convictions. He hired the only hall in town and went to Boston with his chaise every Saturday and brought back Dr. Beecher, Dr. John Codman, Dr. Green, or Dr. Ide, all famous orthodox ministers, to preach. This church that he established in due time became the larger and stronger of the two churches and ultimately, I am glad to say, became the United Church of Walpole.

In 1853 and 1854, he represented the town in the legislature in the general court.

My grandmother, Susanna Gay, came from a long line of people who were interested in intellectual work. She was a granddaughter of John Gay, one of the original settlers of Dedham whose grandson, the Reverend Ebenezer Gay, was for sixty years minister at the old Hingham church. The Reverend Ebenezer Gay, my great-uncle, when he graduated from Harvard in the class of 1814, wore a suit of clothes that his mother and sister had spun and woven in their home from wool sheared from their own sheep. My grandmother and her sisters established the first library in the town. Many of the books we still have. It was called the Ladies Literary & Moral Society Library. My grandmother and her husband were very active in religious work, and I remember even as a boy when she was very old, going to Prayer Meetings at her house.

In 1815 my father was born. That was during the administration of James Madison. He was born not far from the center of the town near the Stetson water privilege. The house is still standing. Whether it was built by my grandfather or not, I do not know.

He was educated in the school located not far from my farm near the site of Mingel's house. It was a red schoolhouse. Subsequently, the schoolhouse was moved over on to Washington Street and made into a factory. For a while he went to school in the town of what was then South Dedham, but I cannot imagine for long. Subsequently, he went to a school in Salisbury, Connecticut. But most of his education, I understand, he got at Day's Academy in Wrentham.

His father needed him so it was impossible for him to go to college, and thus he entered the firm of Henry Plimpton & Son. My father at that time wanted to make shovels because they were building railroads and there was a great demand for them, but on account of the boyhood agreement with Oliver Ames, that was not possible in the eyes of my grandfather.

The business of Henry Plimpton & Son prospered. In due course of time, what was called the lower privilege was purchased and turned over to my uncle, Henry Plimpton, to run as a satinette factory; but he could not make it go, and rather than have it fail, my grandfather and my father paid the debts and said no Plimpton or descendant of his would be allowed to fail.

Soon after, my grandfather decided that he would let his two boys have the business, and the firm became C.G. & H.M. Plimpton. The business then had a factory, a trip-hammer shop—they made springs and axles and more or less all sorts of machinery work, employing perhaps 125 men. In those days the relations between owners and the men were very close. In the family of my grandfather and my grandmother were young men learning the trade. Then they would start out in business for themselves. One such young man was my grandfather's brother, Elias Plimpton, who went down to

Litchfield, Maine, and bought the water privilege and built his works there and afterwards flourished. Another, Jacob White, went out and built his works near Troy, New York. He married my grandfather Lewis's sister, Priscilla Lewis.

They say that at one time my grandfather loaded a ship in 1850 with a load of mining tools, but when he got aboard the ship he found a lot of vacant space. He went out and bought oats and corn and grain and filled up all the chinks. The vessel went around Cape Horn on to San Francisco, and they sold the grain for enough to pay for the entire passage of the ship.

As a boy I remember very well going down to the works. I remember once swinging off from a limb out over the water and the limb broke and I sank and I remember coming up once, coming up again, and it seemed as if my whole life came back to me. Fortunately, Horace Speer, a machinist up at the mill, noticed my going down and pulled me out; otherwise I certainly would have drowned. It is a sensation I shall never forget.

Once a year they used to draw the water out of the pond and they would catch fish and turtles, and then they would have a picnic for the whole day and they would cook the fish and turtles and have a great feast, and they would roll ninepins and do all sorts of feats that were customary in those days.

I remember very well, when Fort Sumter was fired upon they raised a great flag pole and swung out the flag showing their loyalty for the country. I remember there was a company of men who had enlisted from my father's works. I remember how my father used to load the wagon with pies and all sorts of edible things and take them down to the soldiers, and I remember his going from one tent to another and leaving these things for them.

When the Norfolk County Railroad was built, my father and my grandfather gave the railroad about four or five thousand dollars' worth of material, and they were going to take their pay in stock of the railroad. They had the privilege of seeing the railroad built and the name Plimptonville given to designate the village, but the stock was of no value whatever.

On November 20, 1840, my father married Priscilla G. Lewis of Walpole. She was the daughter of Jason Lewis and Ruth Wilkinson Lewis, and most of their farm was in Plimptonville. My father and mother went to the same school. Subsequently, she went to Wheaton College at Norton, Massachusetts. Her oldest sister went to Ipswich to a school kept by

The Lewis Farm, Walpole, Massachusetts; Thanksgiving Day, 1902

Miss Grant and Mary Lyon, but Mary Lyon went on to Wheaton College and from there to Mount Holyoke. It was while Miss Lyon was at Wheaton College that my mother studied there.

Subsequently, my mother taught school at South Walpole, and among her pupils was Albert S. Boyden, who later for sixty years was the principal of the Bridgewater State Normal School. At the celebration given in his honor by the town of Walpole, he stated that he got his inspiration from and owed everything to my mother.

My father built his house in 1839 with four Doric columns in front and went directly from his wedding to this house, and in that house were born eight of the nine children. I was the sixth, three girls and two boys before me, three boys after. This house was destroyed by fire Monday morning, January 22, 1862. I well remember that night. There was a tremendous snowstorm. I heard the word "fire" and it had started in the barn—house and barn were attached, and I remember putting on my brother Edward's clothes and he getting into mine. My mother had pneumonia and they carried her out on a bed, and my sister Idella was ill. It was impossible to get any fire engine there on account of the snow. At that time fire engines were operated by hand. The last thing that my father ordered was that those four columns should be knocked from the house. They succeeded in doing it. Those four columns were saved. I remember my sister Priscilla saving the piano by insisting that the men push it through the window. It was supposed that the fire was started by a discharged mechanic who subsequently proved to have a very bad character, and who ended his days in gaol.

At that time we all relocated to my mother's house, the Lewis Farm, that had been in my mother's family since 1729. In this house my brother Howard was born. A new and greater house was built to replace the old. Father was most anxious to locate the new house on the hill behind, but Mother felt it would be lonesome so far from the street. Finally it was placed on the site of the old house. The new house was of the French roof style and when it was built, it is said, it was the largest house in Norfolk County. The four columns that were saved held up the piazza, two on each side. The doors in the house are of solid Santo Domingo mahogany. While my father was building this house they were tearing down the Rufus Choate house in Boston, and it is said my father bought all the Choate mahogany doors for nine dollars. At that time there were nine children, and my father was determined to have a house large enough to take care of them all.

In the upper part of the house he built a hall to provide for dancing for the children, for their entertainment. One time when they installed a minister in the church, there was no place large enough to give the delegates a place to have their luncheon, and this hall was used for that purpose, bringing the people from the church in carriages.

In 1865 my father was showing a piece of machinery to a friend and kicked off the belt, and unfortunately he got entangled in it and his leg was crushed. I remember as a boy seeing an express wagon drawn by a lot of men with my father in it coming up to the house, and I remember as they drew the stretcher out he said to my mother, "I am coming up to stay with you for a while." But he did not realize his condition. In those days such a thing as an antiseptic did not exist and amortorization set in, and the result was that his leg had to be amputated and he failed to recover. He left a great heritage to a family of nine children—a good name. My father was loved by everybody. I do not suppose one could go into a house in those days without finding my father's picture.

Here are two letters written to me about my father. One is from J. S. Allen, my father's bookkeeper; the other is from George H. Richards, an old iron merchant.

George A. Plimpton, Esq.
New York

My Dear Friend,

I am in receipt of your favor of the 6th inst. in which you ask me to "jot down any impressions I may have of your father as a citizen, as an employer of labor, and etc." The firm of C.G. & H.M. Plimpton was the successor of your grandfather Henry Plimpton, who in 1816 purchased the upper privilege and commenced the manufacture of hoes. In 1844 he purchased the lower privilege with the buildings and machinery which had previously been used by Daniel Ellis & Son in the manufacture of satinets. Soon after this purchase, your uncle Henry engaged in the manufacture of cloth for a year or two, when, owing to the failure of the commission merchants who sold his goods, he gave up the manufacture and soon after, your grandfather having retired from active business, went into company with your father, using both privileges in extending the manufacture of hoes to that of wagon-axles, carriage-springs, iron bars, and other articles of iron and steel. Commencing in 1850, I was for fifteen years in their employ as clerk and general superintendent or overseer of the works. Our relations with each other during these years were always of the most pleasant nature.

At the time I entered their employ, their extensive and lucrative trade with California had commenced. They were receiving large orders from there for hoes, axles, springs, picks, shovels, etc., etc. They made at that time large hoes with long handles used for mining purposes. We used to put them up all bundled in large cases with oats or other kinds of grain, and the profits on the grain would pay the freight on the whole. You say that the methods of doing business in those days were very different from what they are now. There was one method they were led to adopt which was a little peculiar for those days, but which proved to be a very safe method. The goods they sold to California were shipped by sailing vessels around Cape Horn. Consequently they were obliged to give extremely long credits. These notes were given by their customers in California to Geo. C. Johnson & Co., Conrey & O'Conner Treadwell & Co., and others whose names I do not now recall, usually on six or nine months. These notes they would get discounted at the bank to obtain the cash to run their business. Soon after I was with them, your father took one of these notes to the bank for discount. The cashier thinking, I suppose, that they were doing rather a risky business, seemed to hesitate about discounting the note. "Don't you care to discount this note?" says your father.

"I think I had rather not," said the cashier.

"Very well," said your father, "This is the last note I shall ask you to discount." When he came home he said he did not like this getting discounts on notes, and he thought a way might be arranged so that they could carry on their business without being dependent on the banks. They then made arrangements with their customers, that in giving their notes instead of having them made payable to the order of C.G. & H.M. Plimpton, they be made payable to their *own* order. They would then say to the parties from whom they bought their stock, "We are in want of a lot of stock of iron, steel, etc. You may sell it to us on account, or here is a note of Geo. C. Johnson & Co. payable to their own order and endorsed by them which you can have, or you need not sell it to us at all." Of course they wanted to sell the stock and invariably would take the note. The result was that they were able to carry on their business without giving or endorsing or discounting any notes.

As a citizen, manufacturer, and employer of labor, your father was held in high regard and esteem, I believe, by all with whom he came into contact, and by his death and the final consequent closing-up of the business the town as well as his employees lost a good deal of what would have been for their financial interest. As an employer of labor he was ever careful of the welfare of his employees. Most of his help were men of families—good citizens. They were paid good, fair wages and were paid promptly. There were very few complaints and strikes were unknown. He had a peculiar tact in the management of his workmen. One incident among many which came under my observation I will relate: The hands were in the habit, occasionally, of spending the noon hour in pitching quoits. One day there was need of hurry in order to get off a lot of goods that were to be shipped that night. The help, getting a little excited in the game, continued to pitch after the noon hour. Your father coming down and finding them thus engaged, no doubt felt a little mad inside, but instead of speaking crossly, finding fault, or threatening to discharge them, he very quietly went in to pitching with them. After a short time, he said to them, "Now, boys, this won't hardly do. These goods we want to get out to ship tonight and you will have need to hurry." Each man dropped his quoit instantly and rushed to his work, and the goods were ready in season. It was by his tactful acts like this and by his kindness to those under him that he obtained their good will and their willingness to aid him in their labors.

I believe that if employers today were governed more by the same principles that actuated him, there would be less strikes and less troubles than now exist between them and their employees. I have thus hastily written out a few impressions. In looking back over the fifteen years of my connection with the firm, I think I can say that they were among the pleasantest years of my life.

Very sincerely yours,
Samuel Allen

The letter from George H. Richards reads as follows:

Mr. Geo. A. Plimpton

Dear son of my old friend,

I will now try, as you request, to jot down some recollections of your father, but I am afraid that you will get little but the desultory garrulity of an old, old man. I wish I could give you a faithful pen-picture of your father as I knew him, but the day has long gone by since I could write anything like a biography that would bear reading.

When your father and I first met in the '40s, it was a case of "love at first sight"; as the saying is, "we froze to each other," and we never thawed apart. When we were among strangers we were often taken for brothers. Neither we nor any of our families could see the slightest resemblance. We were both tall and, like most mechanics, round shouldered, but there the resemblance ceased. We both had the Dedham "Gay" blood in our veins, and I concluded that we had both inherited some Gay habit of walking or standing or some poise of the head or something that a stranger would notice.

You say you would like to hear what your grandfather told me of the beginning of the Plimpton Iron Works. Your grandfather told me that he and O. Ames were both apprentices in the same hoe shop. When they became of age, your grandfather started in a small way making hoes at the water privilege that afterwards became Plimptonville. I think that he told me that he threw the dam across the river that the public road passed over, but I am not sure about that. If I recollect right, he started in business the year I was born, 1816. Mr. Ames started at the same time in N. Easton making shovels because there was not demand enough for hoes to allow for two more hoe manufacturers. There was a much lighter demand for shovels at that time than for hoes, and for some years your grandfather went ahead of Ames. But Ames made a comfortable living and something more, and paid particular attention to the quality of his shovels, not allowing a poor one to leave his shop. Your grandfather did the same, and in time the O. Ames shovel and the Plimpton hoe were called the *best* in the market, the sale of shovels being so small that everyone thought that your grandfather would become a richer man than Ames. But "Man proposes, and the advance of civilization disposes." In the '30s we began to build railroads. The O. Ames shovel, being the best, had an enormous demand spring up for it, and Oakes Ames, the son of your grandfather's co-apprentice, who was then managing the business, had hard work for several years to satisfy the demand. Then came [the gold rush in] California, which increased the demand for the O. Ames shovel immensely. I recollect that one day in California times I was dining at a restaurant with Oakes Ames, and I asked him how many shovels he was turning out per week. He answered, "Four thousand dozen." "How much does the O. Ames shovel bring over any other make?" "One dollar per dozen," said he. "Then," said I, "if your competitors are selling at cost, you are making four thousand dollars a week." "It looks that way," said Ames.

In the meantime the country had been settling up by the farmers and others moving west; and the further west they got and the smoother the land they worked made a less and less demand for hoes, while the demand for shovels kept on increasing. Here in Illinois we only use a hoe to scratch a little in the garden and flower beds. I have bought but four hoes in over forty years. Even in New England demand for hoes fell off, for many of the farms were deserted or laid down to grass. So you see that by the time your father got old enough to take hold of the business with your grandfather, the business had fallen off so that something had to be done, and your father began to make iron axletrees, crowbars, etc., etc., to piece out the business. Your uncle Henry had by this time come on the carpet, and your grandfather bought a small woolen mill that stood just below the hoe shop and started him in the woolen business. It did not pay very well, but after some years the commission merchant who sold your uncle Henry's goods made a bad failure so that it swamped Henry. He wanted to stop payment and make a compromise, but both your father and grandfather said, "No! Every one of our name must pay his honest debts"; and at very great inconvenience to themselves, they paid Henry's debts, took the woolen machinery out of the mill, and put in lathes and other tools for making axletrees, and your uncle Henry went to work at one of the lathes. I remember that shortly after this was done, I was going through the shop with your father. When we came to the lathe where Henry was working, your father laughed and said, "As soon as Henry can get his hands dirty and not make too bad a face about it, he is going into business with me." Your uncle Henry did hate dust and dirt. He wanted everything "nice."

After this, for some years your father carried on a gradually increasing and profitable business, but his chronic complaint, the asthma, kept increasing on him, and in the spring of 1851 it was so bad that something had to be done. I had been in business with my brother in the iron trade for several years, and confinement to the countingroom had broken me down so that the doctors said I must go back to an unmiasmatic country and spend the summer there in the open air. I had heart trouble. The doctors said it was the relic of a miasmatic shock I had had in the swamps of Arkansas years before. When I told your father that I was going to spend the summer in the West, he said that he would go with me, so we started, spent a week among the anthracite mines in Pennsylvania, and traveled by canal and rivers to Alten, Illinois. Thence by wagon to Hillsboro, where we stayed with an old friend of mine, Mr. A. Lawyer. We lounged around, rode horseback, went hunting for deer—saw some, but didn't get any ourselves—and both of us recovered our health and felt quite well. Your father had no touch of asthma while in Illinois. There were no railroads then, but it was plain that they would come in a few years, and your father proposed to me to get hold of a body of land, and he would move his works out here and his workmen, and I could peddle out the land in small pieces, and [we would] both do well and enjoy better health than in Massachusetts. As soon as Mr. Lawyer heard this talk, he said, "Why here is just the body of land you want. Here is three thousand acres belonging to Dr. Shurtleff's (of Boston) heirs, and they want to sell." He took us all over the land. It joined the town of Hillsboro, and quite a lot of it was in the town plot, and we both concluded that if we could get the land at a reasonable price we would make the move. When we returned to Boston, we called on Dr. Shurtleff, son of the old doctor, who was executor of the estate, and he said they would sell the land at five dollars an acre. We agreed to take it, and he said he would have the deeds ready in a couple of weeks. On calling for the deeds, he said that one of the heirs would not sell under $5.50 per acre, and that they had all come to the same conclusion. Naturally we got mad and bid him good day, thinking that they would come to our terms as they had been trying vainly to sell for some years. Whether they would have done so, I cannot say, for before we heard from them something happened that upset the whole scheme. . . .

Had we been able to have carried out our plan and moved the works to Hillsboro, I think that in all probability your father would have been living today and you boys differently employed, for the railroad came in a few years, and the works would have grown into a gigantic agricultural machine works rivaling McCormack's. When the railroad came to Hillsboro a few years after we were there, the company wanted the town to give land for a depot and repair shops; but as the charter compelled the 'road to come to Hillsboro, the citizens would not only give the company no land but wanted an exorbitant price for it, so the company went twelve miles north of Hillsboro and bought a tract of prairie, laid out the town of Litchfield, and put the repair shops there. The course of the railroad was southwest. Just outside the town they turned northwest and just touched the limits of the town on the north, half a mile from the courthouse, thence on till farther north to Litchfield, thence south to the proper course, thus making the 'road seventeen miles longer than it need have been. Had your father been here, the 'road would have got the land it wanted. As it turned out, after some years the 'road had to move their repair shop to Mattoon owing to lack of water in Litchfield in dry years. Hillsboro has an abundance of water at all times. All our land here has a nine-foot vein of coal under it. It thins out to less than four feet in Litchfield. Your father used often to speak regretfully of the choice that his father and O. Ames made when they first started in the business. I used to tell him that Ames was not a prophet nor the son of a prophet, and that our western hunters used to say that if a man's foresight was as good as his hindsight he would always be successful.

A short distance below your father's works, a Mr. F. W. Bird had a water power and paper mill. He was a queer, lob-sided, one-idea man. Every man that did not think as he did was an enemy and a fool. When Mr. Bird joined the Free Soil Democratic combination, your father came under that category, and Mr. Bird opposed him in everything he did—town matters, school matters, etc., etc.—and, strange to say, though your father's men would go through fire and water for him, if there was a chance to vote on any subject that was of no very great importance they would always vote for Mr. Bird's proposition, and Mr. Bird's men would vote on your father's side. There was a schoolhouse between Plimptonville and Bird's mill, used by both. Bird got up a plan to move it nearer him. Bird employed but a few men, your father many, and Bird carried the day, your father's men voting to have their children wade in the snow, mud, and storm further than they were doing, just to show their "independence." A year or two afterwards, Bird did or said something to offend your father's men, and the schoolhouse was moved back; but it was not long before Bird got another vote, and had it moved over again. It was comical, and your father had many a good laugh over it.

One day when your father was in Boston, the roof of the old woolen factory caught fire. It was used then as a machine shop. The men came out but had no way of putting out the fire, and began moving out the tools. Just then one of the trip-hammer men, Mr. Booth, came up from the forge and gave the men a good dressing, said the fire had got to be put out, and ordered them to get buckets and pass water up to him. He scrambled out on the roof and succeeded at the risk of his life in putting out the fire. Had there been a carpenter or a slater there, nothing would have been heard of taking out the tools and letting it burn; but for a man who couldn't get ten feet off the ground without being dizzy, it was a bold thing to do.

Your father always wanted to put up a rolling mill but never saw his way clear to do it. When a young man, he worked for some time in Connecticut to learn the trade. He was a better workman at any part of the business than any of his men. One day when I was going through the shops with him, he stopped to speak to a man who was trimming with shears the edges of hoes. I remarked that I wanted just such a pair of shears and asked where they were sold. Your father said, "Come along and I will show you." We went into the trip-hammer shop. He took a piece of steel to the fire, thence to the hammer, and forged out a pair in a few minutes. Then he tempered them and handed them to a grinder to sharpen and to put in the rivet. I carried the shears home that evening, and I have them yet in my shop. Money would not buy them.

Your father always liked a good fast horse and always kept one. One that I recollect that he called "Old Indian" he drove to Boston and back in the same day, three times a week for several years. I never liked a fast horse. I kept a slow steady one that a child could drive, called "Old Jim." When your father would go out to Jamaica Plain with me to pass the night, he would make all manner of fun of Old Jim. When I moved to Hillsboro I could not bear to sell the horse, so with your father's permission, I gave him to [your neighbor] Fritta. Your father renamed him "Ethan Allen," the name of the fastest trotter of the day, and I dare say made poor Fritta's life a burden as long as Old Jim lived, bragging about his speed. When he came out here in November, 1860, he told me about Fritta's fast driving.

When the Civil War broke out we had more Copperhead than Union men in this end of the state, and everyone expected trouble. Your father, knowing that I had no arms, and that they could not be got out here, sent me a pair of Navy revolvers and a Cavalry U.S. flag. To get the flag, he bought some bunting and your mother and sisters sewed it together and sewed on cloth stars. We Union men sent all the boys to the war, the Copperheads armed and drilled, and we old folks got up a cavalry regiment of Home Guards, six hundred strong, and paraded at short intervals all over the country. Your father's flag was the flag of the regiment. We were thoroughly drilled and kept the Coppers down. We saw no actual service except a two days' chase after a band of Missouri guerrillas. After the war was over I took the flag from the color sergeant and have it yet, my only war relic.

So to wind up these random recollections of your father, I will say that the pleasantest thought I have is that it can now be but a short time before I shall meet him again.

Yours truly,
Geo. H. Richards
April 1899

On the death of my father, a tremendous responsibility rested upon my mother—the bringing up of the six boys and three girls, the oldest one not over twelve. But she was equal to the situation.

In the first place, she believed firmly in character. She herself was a strong Christian character, and she believed that education and religion should go hand in hand. One of the first things she did was to sell the works. People thought it was a dreadful thing, for the profits were large, but she was not a businesswoman and with nine children had all she could manage. It was sold as a corporation called the Plimpton Iron & Steel Company to a family by the name of Tilton. Against her own judgment, she kept a few shares in the company because it had been established by her husband's father. Fortunately, before it was too late, she sold her interest. She kept the old homestead and the house and whatever land was necessary. She discharged all the men on the farm and took my oldest brother, John, and said, "Now, John, I am going to hold you responsible for running this place and you will have your brothers to help you." She thought it was much better for her to keep the old homestead with all the associations rather than to go to Cambridge, where her friends urged her to take a house and be near good schools and near a college. She said, "What is there for my children to do when they are out of school?" The result was that each of the boys in turn became sort of a farmer; we all learned how to milk, how to raise crops of various sorts, how

Five of the six Plimpton brothers: George, Edward, John, Herbert, and Lewis

to do simple carpentering, make all kinds of tools, have lots of practical experience—and I cannot imagine a better training for a boy to have than that my brothers and I had.

Our great treat when we had got in the last load of hay was to take the old tent that had come down from the Walpole Light Infantry, load a wagon with food, pots, and kettles, and go to Squantum beyond Quincy to camp, fish, dig clams, and swim in salt water. It was a great sport for us, and coming home we would bring clams for ourselves and all the neighbors.

Always in the evening when we had a party, we would have molasses candy, nuts gathered in the fall, shagbarks and butternuts, apples, and pop-corn before the open fireplaces. Oftentimes in winter we would take the big sled, put seats or hay in the center, get all the boys and girls, and go off for a long sleigh-ride on moonlight nights. In winter there was skating and hockey, with bonfires on the ice. We never went to dancing parties. Mother thought their influence was bad, as Tom, Dick, and Harry went to them. The Orthodox people in the church we went to did not believe in dancing or

Frances Taylor Pearsons and George Arthur Plimpton

card-playing. We were brought up to know the value of money. Our associations and pleasures were all connected with the church. The great occasions for the boys were the Christmas tree, the strawberry festival, and the picnics, etc. My mother never let an opportunity go by when she could get some wandering minister or returned missionary or some visiting preacher to come to the house.

During the summer, Walpole was the headquarters for my cousins, my mother's sisters' families who came from Springfield—the Vails, the Hicksons, and the Crossacks—and there were a lot of them. Thanksgiving was our great family gathering.

CHAPTER II

My boyhood days were similar to those of other boys living in the country. In addition to doing the chores in the barn and on the farm, I used to set snares to catch rabbits and traps to catch muskrats. Occasionally we would catch a mink whose skin we would sell to bring us a little "in-money."

The high school was a mile-and-a-half from home. We walked that each day. Occasionally we would get a ride on a railroad train, and sometimes we would take the boat and row up as far as Stetson's Dam, but usually we walked. There was a group of us boys: Edmund Grover, William Everett, Charles S. Bird, Edmund Winslow, Byron Piper, and my brothers Lewis and Edward. So we usually had companions both ways.

At the high school we had Latin. The Latin grammar used was Andrews and Stoddard. My brother Lewis committed to heart the entire Latin grammar with all the illustrations. I oftentimes had to hold the book while he did this. In 1869 he went to Phillips Exeter Academy and roomed with a boy from East Walpole by the name of Charlie Place.

Previously I had visited my sister, Mrs. Adams, at Andover, and seeing the boys there fired me with the ambition to go. The following year, in 1870, I went with my brother to Exeter. I remember perfectly the sensations I had in leaving home. I went by the Norfolk County Railroad. At Dedham we changed cars, for that was the end of the 'road. Somehow or other I felt I was leaving home for all time.

At Phillips Academy I was admitted by Dr. Soule, who expressed surprise that I was so big for my age. He taught Latin. Professor Wentworth taught Mathematics and Professor Cilley taught Greek. These were three remarkable teachers. The first term we had Latin three times a day and Roman History on Monday morning. There were two buildings: the old Academy building and Abbot Hall, the dormitory. I roomed with my brother. We took care of our room ourselves. We had an air-tight stove for which we bought and cut our own wood. There was no bathroom and our toilet was outdoors some little distance from the hall. We had our meals in the building, and I remember how on Monday mornings we were all up and standing on the steps waiting for the breakfast bell to ring. On Monday mornings we had beans that had been left over from the previous Sunday and warmed over, and the supply was limited to those who got there first.

It was during the winter that the old Academy building was burned. I remember that there was a fine old tall clock in it that I wanted to save, but I found it impossible to do so.

The only means of exercise we had were one set of parallel bars and a place for a giant swing. The only athletics we had was after evening prayers when the school divided itself into East and West and kicked football. It was association game where you were not allowed to touch the ball. If Dr. Soule should come on the ground while we were playing, everyone would stop until he passed off. He was a fine type of old gentleman and very dignified.

After I had been at Exeter nearly two years, I realized how expensive it was and planned to see if I couldn't save a year. I found that I had Latin and Greek enough and English and History enough so that I could enter Amherst College. I was not a particularly bright scholar. Things came hard to me, but I had confidence that with a little extra study I could make the examination. There were two others besides myself who wished to save a year: one was George Cumming and the other Herbert Greene, both of whom were subsequently graduated at Harvard.

I took two letters to Amherst and, arriving there about four weeks before the time of the entrance examination, got George Adams, a junior, to coach me. I had never studied geometry. Two books of Lommis were required; so, about a week or ten days before the examination, I committed those two books to memory. I successfully passed the examinations, with the exception that I was conditioned in spelling. That was in 1872, the year that Amherst won the intercollegiate boat race on the Connecticut River.*

---

*George Arthur Plimpton's grandson, Francis T. P. Plimpton, Jr., started the revival of rowing in 1947 and was captain of the crew in 1950.

Before leaving Amherst, I visited the different college fraternities and was pledged to DKE by Melvil Dewey. What influenced me to go to Amherst was first to save a year at Exeter, and second because I desired the benefit of the instruction in English by Professor Clark Seeley, whose instruction, however, I never received, since he became the president of Smith College. During the summer I spent most of my time with spelling books, with which I was more or less occupied day and night even when I was away. In the fall when I took the examinations, I again failed miserably. However, I was so good in other subjects that when I had my final oral examinations, such words were given to me as "cat," "horse," or "dog," so that I finally matriculated and was a full-fledged member of the student body, without condition.

The president of the college at that time was W. A. Stearns, a graduate of Harvard and a fine Christian gentleman who had served as pastor of a church at Cambridge, Massachusetts. He succeeded Dr. Edward Hitchcock, the famous geologist. Professor Julius K. Seeley taught Philosophy. He was a magnificent man physically and intellectually. He was also a most inspiring teacher who used the Socratic method and who subsequently became president of Amherst. Physics was taught by Professor Ebenezer Snell, who was a member of the first class to be graduated from Amherst College and who edited Omstead's *Philosophy.* Those were the days when electricity was interesting but of no earthly use to anybody. I had Professor Esty in Mathematics and also tutor Leud, but Mathematics was very hard, especially geometry. Fortunately for me the days of original examples in geometry were over, for with my knowledge obtained largely by memorization, I should have been terribly handicapped otherwise. Even as it was, the subject was very difficult. Even in my dreams it became a sort of nightmare if, when I was sent to the board to make a demonstration, I would forget the previous reasoning. I do not recommend to anyone to follow my doings.

One of the most interesting courses I had at Amherst was under John W. Burgess on the development of constitutional government. He laid before us the backbone of the history of civilization as a sort of skeleton, and it has been of the greatest service to me all the days of my life. He began back in the Middle Ages and came down more or less to the present time. Whatever has been learned of history since has a place where it can be put. It was my greatest regret and a great loss to the college when in my senior year he left Amherst to go to Columbia University.

The Reverend Humphery Niel taught English Literature. He had been a minister and settled over a church. The textbook we used was Shaw's *English Literature.* I always felt as if we began the study together, as a new experience for him as well as for myself. We studied about authors but did not read their works. We studied about Shakespeare but did not read his plays.

In Greek we had Professor Tyler, a dear, good old man. It was an inspiration to sit at his feet. He loved the Greek authors. They were a part of his life, and you could not but catch his enthusiasm for them. He didn't care so much about the grammar, but he did want us to catch the spirit of what the authors wrote about.

In Latin we had Professor Crowell, an exacting scholar who cared more for the grammar than Tyler did. Later he became blind but still taught to the greatest satisfaction of his pupils.

Professor Mather also taught us Greek. He always seemed to us, notwithstanding he was a minister, worldly wise. He had traveled a good deal and knew much about art. In fact, he established the collection of sculpture at Amherst.

Dr. Hitchcock, the son of the grand old president of Amherst, was the first to teach Physical Culture at Amherst. In fact, he was the first man to take care of the first college gymnasium built in this country. Once a day each class appeared in the gymnasium and went through regular class exercises with dumbbells. I can see him today with a book from which he used to call the roll, slapping it to the music of the piano. He was whole-souled and generous in overlooking the faults of the men. Many a boy would never have been graduated at Amherst had it not been for Dr. Hitchcock's interest in him. He certainly was a student's friend.

Professor Emerson taught us Geology. He was a most genial soul, known from one end of the world to the other as a great geologist. When we built the Fairweather Building, he had a balcony added to his room from which he could point out the different ages in the world's geological history.

Professor Montague taught us French. He, too, was a good old soul and had a good knowledge of French, but he was not a good teacher.

With hardly an exception, all the faculty of Amherst were ministers. They supplemented their income by preaching on Sundays. Without exception, they were all strong Christian men and took great interest in the religious welfare of the students. Almost every year there was a revival.

My first term at Amherst I lived in the room in the old house that had formerly belonged to President Hitchcock. I had as roommate a man named Frank Bowler. He was helped through Exeter by a man in Fall River named Reminton who paid his expenses at Amherst. We remained together only one term. He dressed well, had plenty of money, and never seemed to appreciate what was done for him.

At the end of my first term I was paying, I think, four or five dollars for my board. Knowing that my mother was at great expense to keep me there, I used to contrive ways to earn money. There were clubs where the men got together and brought the board to very much less. I thought I would see what I could do, so I found a man named Celand and got him to open up a house. I agreed to get twenty-two or twenty-three boys, and we would figure up what compensation he and his wife would need. They would do the cooking and I would furnish the food, dividing up the expenses *pro rata* amongst the boys. I bought some of my provisions in Boston, meats in Amherst, and made a study of diet. The result was that I got the board down to $2.50 for each boy. I ran that club until the end of my junior year. I used to give them oatmeal for breakfast and would use such coarse granulated sugar that it would roll off the spoon back into the sugar bowl before it got into the oatmeal, so there was quite a saving in sugar, which was more expensive then than now. Another favorite dish was oysters put up with crackers, which made scalloped oysters with a few oysters and lots of cracker crumbs. This was a very cheap dish and the men were very fond of it. Sometimes I bought a whole sheep. But at the end of my junior year I was sick of it, and lived at the hotel, I believe, all the rest of the time.

Along about the beginning of each college term I used to get up a placard giving the hours of arrival and departure of trains, post office information, and other information about the college and various events during the year. Around the placard would be a lot of advertisements, enough to pay for the printing. I would slip these placards under the doors of the men and thus earn fifty or sixty dollars each year. I never told anybody who did it.

I wrote a guide book to the buildings and museums of Amherst College, and in this I associated myself with a classmate named Beardsley. He was a good scholar, and since I was terribly afraid I would make some spelling or grammatical mistake, he would look out for that. After the book was printed to the number of some fifteen hundred copies, I got testimonials from the faculty, and with a good circular I placed them on the seats in morning chapel, thereby creating a great interest among the student body in regard to it. I then got the professors to let me go before each class to ask for subscriptions at fifty cents for one book or three books for a dollar. The result was that I sold almost the whole edition before any student had seen a copy, and thereby I made about four hundred dollars—my first venture in the publishing business. But I could not have done it had I not obtained a lot of advertising. I had tried to get the trustees to make an appropriation, but no one had ever published anything connected with that college that had not proved a loss. That is why I resorted to advertising. I remember that when the books were all printed, there was a mistake on the title page—they left the "s" out of "museum." I kicked and tossed all night feeling that such a mistake would follow me all the days of my life. But about three or four o'clock, I said to myself, "I bet nobody will notice it" and turned over and went to sleep, and so it proved and I never mentioned it myself.

We graduated a class of seventy-six. There were some very brilliant men who became ministers, doctors, and lawyers. Out of the seventy-six who were graduated, there are not many more than eighteen or nineteen who are alive today in 1933.

As I look back over my college course, I should like to have had a good tutoring in finance and economics. We had nothing of that sort, not even political economy. We didn't even have a course in history, with the exception of what Professor Burgess gave us. Professor Seeley taught us Hickock's Moral Philosophy and Hickock's Mental Philosophy. Two definitions also come back to me after all these years: "Sensation is the identification of the reciprocal modification of both the recipient organ and the thing received"; and "Mind is the conscious perduring of a somewhat as opposed to entity."

I got a good deal of pleasure and profit out of DKE. The society was made up of members of my own class, about ten or twelve sophomores and seniors. The success of DKE depended on getting the best men in each class: the best scholars, the best athletes, and the best all-around men. My classmates were all fine men. Beardsley became a famous preacher but died early. Knight became salutatorian of our class and subsequently professor at the Hartford Theological Seminary. McGeorge Bundy became a lawyer whose wife took all his money and deserted him. George Guild became a minister at Scranton, Pennsylvania. Greene became a New York City public school teacher.

The clubhouse was in Phoenix Row. There were one or two bedrooms connected with it, and I occupied one of them with my brother Edward while he was there. As I look back on it now, it was a miserable way to live, but it was economical and I was strong and well and did not mind it. While in college I never held any office and never won any prizes. The greatest honor that ever came to me was this: We had two societies, the Alexander and the Athens. I was fortunate enough to be one of the orators, and I remember wearing my brother's Prince Albert coat and patent leather shoes, which made a tremendous squeak when I walked on the platform. My sister Idylla was there and saw that I had some flowers. I didn't come near to getting any of the prizes.

My brother Edward entered Amherst in 1874 and was in the class of 1878. His first two years we roomed together.

He is also a member of DKE, and he succeeded in winning a prize at Amherst by swinging Indian clubs. He also became a famous baseball player. He played first base on the Amherst nine and in fact made a great reputation. Even now I occasionally meet people who say, "Aren't you the Plimpton who was the famous baseball player at Amherst?" One summer he played first base on a team in western New York. On this team were two of my classmates: Stalk, who lived at Auburn, and John B. Stanchfield, who afterwards became a famous criminal lawyer and was the man who invented the twist in pitching the ball.

CHAPTER III

After I had finished college, I was very anxious to go to the Centennial, but I was loath to ask my mother for the money. So I looked around to see if I could earn some money. We are all of us more or less creatures of accident—happening to meet Melvil Dewey on the street near the corner of Beacon and Tremont Streets in Boston, he asked me to accompany him while he saw Mr. Ginn a moment. Mr. Ginn was the head of Ginn & Company, textbook publishers. Mr. Dewey had known Mr. Ginn for some time, as a friend of his had put into Mr. Dewey's hands some money to invest and he had loaned it to Mr. Ginn. This was greatly appreciated at the time. It was in relation to this that Mr. Dewey called. Upon being introduced to him, Mr. Ginn asked me what I was planning to do. I said I was planning to go to Harvard Law School in the fall, but in the meantime I wished to earn some money to go to the Centennial. He called up Mr. E. O. Fisk, who had been working for him about a year, to explain to me the nature of the business. He told me about the schoolbooks and what it was necessary to do. The terms, Mr. Ginn said, would be fifty percent of what I sold. I would pay my own expenses and furnish my own money. Hearing what schoolbook selling was all about, at first I was not inclined, because two or three summers before I had spent some days selling a subscription book—the *Sermons of Adirondack Murray*—and that had been enough bookselling for me. He said, "Let me introduce you to our agent, Fisher, and you talk to him." I decided I would like to try it, and Mr. Ginn suggested that I take my home town, Walpole, and the neighboring towns, Sharon and Foxboro. Thinking that the business was connected more or less with ordinary book business by subscription, I hesitated. "Can't I have some territory near the World's Exposition near Philadelphia?" I asked. He very strongly objected. But as I persisted and as there was no agent there, he reluctantly said I might have that territory. So with a lot of books—our world geographies, Arnold's *English Literature,* and our Latin books—I packed all I could carry, bid him goodbye, and bought a ticket to New York and from there to York, Pennsylvania.

I took the train to the Fall River boat and occupied the

seat with a man whose name I have forgotten. He told me he manufactured needles and lived in North Cambridge. He learned I was starting out on this trip for the first time and asked me if I would not share his stateroom with him, as he had a vacant berth. Just before retiring he said it was his custom always to read aloud a chapter in the Bible and asked me if I wouldn't pick out my favorite chapter to read, which was rather embarrassing as I had no favorite chapter. However, I picked one out, and after I had finished reading it, he offered up a prayer. I remember distinctly this prayer, which was on the theme of "this young man is going out into the world. . . . He has no idea of the sort of temptations he will be subjected to." He then named some of these temptations. He asked the Lord with all his fervor to protect me against them, and that if I did get them to give me power to resist them. While at Harvard Law School I called on him, as he was a deacon in the Old Church at North Cambridge.

I landed at York, Pennsylvania, where the language of the people was Dutch. In fact, the whole section in which I worked was amongst the Pennsylvania Dutch. I did some business, however, with the York Academy and in Lancaster. I visited the coal regions where the trials of the Molly McGuires, a secret organization, had just ended. Here a detective by the name of McPalen had exposed the whole thing. The story of his work reads like a romance. I remember walking past Professor Nevin's house at Franklin and Marshall College four or five times before I had the courage to ring the doorbell. I remember to my amazement that I was most cordially received, and he told me that he would use my Arnold's *English Literature* with his next class. I attended the adoption meeting by the school board in the township of Lancaster in a barroom. I had seen each member and had shown each one my geography, but they voted to take Mitchell's, and the agent treated them to whiskey—this was a new experience for me. However, I was successful in getting our geographies introduced in the city of Phoenixville and also in Coatsville. Having spent two weeks at the Centennial, I returned to Boston, when I had made about $150 net, after paying all my expenses.

CHAPTER IV

I entered Harvard Law School in the fall of 1876 with money that I had saved up, having settled up with Mr. Ginn, although a final settlement was not made until about January. Those were the days when we had little money, and I was in no particular hurry for it. At that time Harvard Law School had some famous teachers. They had what is called the case system. Among the teachers was Ames, who taught the subject of torts. He was a very interesting teacher who followed the Socratic method. The case system was most valuable to me because the decisions of the judges were based largely on what had happened before, so that we would begin at the oldest case and proceed to the subsequent ones. When once we had the facts, we were just as able as the judge to decide questions of the law. I enjoyed this method of study much, and it has been of great use to me in after life. Among the great teachers at Harvard Law School at that time were Langdell, the author of the case system, Gray, and Thayer. Washburn died while we were there. I had a room in a private house and took my meals in Alumni Hall.

Just before the year ended, I saw on the bulletin board a notice that read: "Wanted: An assistant professor to teach History and Political Science at the University of Nebraska. Salary, $1,500. Applications to be made to President Eliot." Since I did not have much money at that time, this seemed to me an ideal opportunity to teach in a university and in the meantime to finish my studies and to grow up in the state of Nebraska. I interviewed President Eliot, who told me that no one had applied and that my chances were fair. Meeting Mr. Ginn on the street afterwards, I told him I had thought of getting this position. Instantly he said, "What is the salary?" I told him. "Oh," he said, "I'll give you more than that if you work for me for a year. I will not only give you your salary, but will also pay your expenses wherever you go." Then the question for me to decide was whether to try for the Nebraska position or to accept Mr. Ginn's offer. The professors at the Law School told me that if I were to practice law, experience in the business world would be of much more value to me than teaching. They said that men failed in law not so much because they did not know law, but because they did not know men, and that therefore the experience of dealing with men would be of the utmost value to me.

The firm at that time had become Ginn & Heath. Mr. Heath had been in the employ of Ginn Brothers, with headquarters in Rochester, New York, for several years, and during the year had been taken into the firm. Mr. Ginn's brother, Frederick B. Ginn, had retired. My headquarters was to be in New York, and Mr. Heath would move from Rochester to Boston. We had desk-room with C. T. Dillingham; that is, we had a place where our mail was received, but subsequently we hired a place at 20 Bond Street next to Macmillan. This served as the headquarters of our New York office for several years. For some time I was the sole representative of the firm west of Boston. Our publications at that time were largely Latin and Greek and music and the Hudson *Shakespeare.* Latin and Greek were used pretty universally, and the best books were Professor Goodwin's *Greek Grammar,* supplemented by John S. White's *Greek Lessons,* which we published. In Latin we had the Allen and Greenough series, which differed from all other grammars in that it taught on a comparative basis. The only common school books we had were the *Our World Geographies,* which combined history and geography. We had the Fitz Globes, the six-inch and the twelve-inch. This globe was so fixed that it showed many features different from all other globes. At the end of the first year, Mr. Ginn said the profits on the sale of the globes were sufficient so that whatever we did with the books was clear gain. Once in Camden, New Jersey, the Board of Education adjourned without purchasing my globes. I felt so bad about it that I couldn't help getting "right up in meeting" and saying, "Gentlemen, you haven't purchased my globes!" The way I said it made such an impression that they reassembled and bought fourteen or fifteen for each schoolhouse. I remember that in my first year I sold enough Fitz Globes to pay my travel and expenses and that all else I made was clear gain. At the end of my first year, Mr. Ginn raised my salary to two thousand dollars; at the end of the second year he made it twenty-four hundred dollars. I had saved twelve hundred dollars by the end of the fourth year in

1881, and he took me into the firm and it became Ginn, Heath & Company—I being the "Company." We had had a house in Chicago, but the representative had just been hired by Appleton to go to New England and, if possible, to take the Ginn books out of every school.

By that time we had strengthened our list considerably. My old teacher Wentworth had published a geometry, the chief characteristic of which was that the figures were on the same page with the text. Soon after this he published an algebra. The great feature of his books was the problems and examples. He believed that you learn to do by doing and was a great advocate of insisting on the fundamental principles being drilled into a boy and then giving him plenty of problems. As he said, "Every tub must stand on its own bottom."

Professor Whitney of Yale wrote us an English grammar, and Mr. Ginn asked me to stop off and talk with him to learn from him the reasons why his book was better than any other. In my interview with him I asked how his essentials of grammar differed from Swinton's, from Greene's, and from the other popular books then in use. He said, "I don't know; I have never seen any of those books." I said, "If this is so, how do you know that the work you have done is not merely a repetition of theirs?" He replied, "I examine the students in English who come to Yale College, and if they had had the training from a book of my sort they would never have made the blunders they have made."

I am quite sure that this must be the only instance of a man having written a textbook without having consulted and examined others.

The first book that Mr. Ginn published was Craik's *English of Shakespeare.* Subsequently he purchased Hudson's *Shakespeare* in three volumes, which had already been published many years. Hudson revised it and brought out a school edition of it. He was a very remarkable man: tall—six feet or more—straight as an arrow. He loved Shakespeare and loved the best in literature. His introduction in his school edition has hardly ever been equalled. This *Shakespeare,* after fifty years, is still very successful. I remember that in the preface to his *Classical English Reader* he says, "Old books, old music, old friends are the books, the music, the friends for me."

Luther Whiting Mason wrote a series of music books while superintendent of music in Cincinnati. It was not successful. The idea was a good one, but it was not in the hands of the proper people for publication. It was offered to Mr. Ginn for a mere song. Mr. Mason came to Boston. The idea was that the teachers, after instruction from his book, could teach the classes from fifteen to twenty minutes a day and that in due time the children would be able to read music. The music books became a great success and brought much money into the firm. It was this series that furnished the "sinews of war" and built up money for the publishing business. It is not necessary here to allude further to the new books and new series that were added to the firm.

Mr. Ginn and Mr. Heath, after they had been together four or five years, did not get along well. They had adjoining offices and would write each other long letters of complaint, sending me copies of each. Finally they came to the point where they had to separate, about 1884 or 1885. Mr. Heath wanted his pay in certain of our publications. He took our science books—Remson's *Chemistry*, Hyatt's series—and the modern languages. Then the question came as to who should take Shelden's *History*. This was written by Miss Shelden, whose father was head of the Normal School at Oswego. It was based on the case system, which required that a lot of supplementary reading be done. It was the history we were all banking on. In fact, it was supposed to make a great sensation. We were all anxious to bet that book. We had previously purchased from Harper Brothers Myers's *General History*. I remember taking Myers's *History* and reading it through. I was so much interested in it that I told Mr. Ginn that this was the book to get and not the Shelden. It was rather difficult to convince him, but after reading chapter after chapter to him he was persuaded that I was right. The two books were put up at auction between us at one time, and Mr. Heath paid a large price for the Shelden while we got the Myers for almost nothing. In the end, the Myers had a great sale and brought in a lot of money for Ginn

& Company. In other words, my prediction proved absolutely correct.

One time while Mr. Ginn was in Europe, we decided to publish a United States history by Montgomery. I read the proof when it was nearly all set up and saw that it was the work of a genius but that in its present form it would never succeed. I got him to submit it to a grammar school teacher and the historical facts to Professor Jameson of Brown University. We reset the book, and when it was finally published it proved to be probably the most profitable book that Ginn & Company ever got out.

I remember once spending a week at Lookout Mountain. Amongst our group was William T. Harris, superintendent of schools in St. Louis, Missouri. I asked him what books he would advise me to read to be a good publisher. He mentioned four authors. It is very seldom that I found anyone better than those four authors. They were Homer, Dante, Shakespeare, and Goethe (*Faust*). He supplemented this advice by saying it wouldn't hurt any to read Hegel's *History of Philosopy*. In other words, what a publisher should have is a good cultural background.

CHAPTER V

My first interest in collecting was aroused at an auction of the household goods and other belongings of Benjamin Lewis, who lived in a nearby house when I was a boy. I went and bought a complete uniform belonging to the Walpole Light Infantry: red coat, tall hat with plume, knapsack, and powder-horn. I remember putting them all on and strutting home proud as Lucifer. I don't believe I was more than eight or nine years old, and I bid it all in for twelve cents. This, I think, was the first of my collecting, and through all of my boyhood days this was the costume that was worn whenever we had theatricals, Fourth of July celebrations such as horribles, etc.

My mother had a cousin, "Mirandy" Guild by name. She lived in an old house right near the Dedham railroad station. Whenever we drove to Boston, we always stopped to see Cousin Mirandy Guild. Sometimes we put up the horse in her barn and took the train, for this was before the New York and New England Railroad was built. She was a collector, and in her parlor she used to show us all sorts of things. I remember she had part of George Washington's coffin. I once gave her a piece of the bell from Phillips Exeter Academy that used to call Daniel Webster to school. She gave me the three-cornered hat that had belonged to her grandfather Captain Aaron Guild, and the sword that her brother had worn in the Mexican War, and she made me notice the bloodstains on the blade, proving that it had been "put to good use." Long afterwards, when she died, she bequeathed these things to her nieces in Westford, and I remember I once went all the way to Westford to see if the things would make the same impression on me that they had when I was a boy. Strange to say, they did not.

My training at the Harvard Law School stimulated me to know something about the early textbooks. What were the first books published as textbooks? I started, in a modest way, trying to gather them together. I remember that the first book I wanted to get was the *New England Primer,* the beginning of reading. I especially hunted for books used in colonial days, for previous to the Revolution nearly all textbooks (with few exceptions) were imported from England. Following those were the readers, such as Sanders' *Readers*. (Even they sold largely in my day, and then the McGuffey *Readers*, the early geographies, and the books on penmanship.) In fact, it was the early American books that I was after. I remember with what glee I found the book printed by Benjamin Franklin called *The Schoolmaster's Assistant*. This book was a sort of encyclopedia of things necessary for a boy to know. There was a chapter on writing, with specimens; a chapter on arithmetic; one on geography; one on grammar; and also some on bookkeeping and law. It was just such a book as that written by a man named Mather that George Washington had studied.

I remember also picking up a *New England Primer* that bore the portrait of George Washington and was printed during the Revolutionary War. This was really the great beginner's book, and the first printed in this country. It grew largely out of the *Royal Primer* and the *Children's Classbook*. Early editions of this book are greatly sought after. I remember a schoolteacher in Bucks County, Pennsylvania, bringing to me a copy of the *New England Primer* printed in 1728, for which he wanted one thousand dollars. This happened to be the earliest *New England Primer* known with date. Commodore Vanderbilt had one, but this antidated it. Subsequently it was sold to Mr. Church of Brooklyn for twenty-five hundred dollars, and from him it was purchased by H. C. Huntington, and it is now in his library in Pasadena. I have altogether about thirty *New England Primers*.

Henry Barnard, the first United States commissioner of education, publisher of *Barnard's Journal*, who lived in Hartford, was also interested in early American textbooks. He had, at that time, the largest collection of *New England Primers*, but none of very early date. He was tremendously interested in my undertaking and helped me by describing the sort of things to look for, and he was a frequent visitor at my home. He was full of reminiscences and a most entertaining talker. He graduated from Yale in 1833 and spent the following year in Washington. He knew Webster, the Clays, and the Calhouns, to whom he paid a visit, stopping all along the way at old Virginia houses, including one night with Monroe at Montpelier. The following year he went to England. He had letters from Webster to the Earl of Ashburnham, met Wordsworth—who recited to him the ode on Tintern Abbey—and Coleridge, and had long talks with Carlyle. He lived to be ninety years old and had a celebration on his birthday. I remember that when he heard I was to be married, he got up, as always, at four in the morning, and came to me to urge me to live the first five years of my married life either in the country or in Brooklyn. He said, "If you live in the city of New York you will have no opportunity to get acquainted with your wife. Her interests and yours will be so diverse that you will see little of each other, whereas if you live in the country, you will necessarily be thrown together, and your interests must be in common." I was unable to follow his advice, but the consequences were not what he feared.

I was fortunate in being able to acquire a great many early books that were used before the Revolution and printed in England, such as Dillworth's (with a quaint portrait of himself), Hodder's arithmetic, and even Cocker's, which had such an extended use in England that the expression "I swear by Cocker" still is prevalent.

Isaac Greenwood, professor at Harvard, wrote a book in 1728 called *The Vulgar Arithmetic*. Harvard College had two copies, one imperfect, which I traded from them. Greenwood had been dismissed for intoxication. Afterwards I purchased another copy with the autograph of Samuel Adams, signer of the Declaration of Independence and called "The Father of the Revolution."

These are a few of the books printed and studied previous to the Revolutionary War. After we gained independence we began to make our own textbooks. Noah Webster wrote his three books, the first in 1783, and I remember the pleasure with which I secured the first. It was in Governor Pennypacker's collection and was sold at auction in Philadelphia. It proved to be the original copy that Noah Webster had presented to Harvard College, and it has the Harvard bookplate. Probably some later librarian had discarded it as having no value. Soon after, I followed this purchase with others of Webster's books, together with a first edition of his old "Blue-backed Spelling Book," of which, until comparatively recently, the sales were a million a year.

Once, in looking through the John Carter Brown Library,* I saw that he had studied an arithmetic printed in the year 1736. I had never seen a copy of that book. For years afterwards I looked for it in all the old bookshops and catalogues. One day a bookseller in Albany received an old lady who brought it in to sell. He bought it and took the next train to New York and sold it to me for $150—the end of long years of search.

In 1784 Jedidiah Morse (Yale, 1783) taught in a girls' school and wrote the first geography printed in America. Morse was afterwards pastor of the old church at Charleston, Massachusetts—the pulpit formerly occupied by John Harvard. His son was the Morse who invented the telegraph.

Soon after this, Caleb Bingham wrote a series of books. He opened a girls' school in Boston.

One day on University Place, in a little old shop kept by a man named Dr. Leori, I bought a manuscript of Rollandus for fifteen dollars. It was on arithmetic. Rollandus was the canon of the St. Chapelle in Paris and wrote his treatise in the year 1424. Charles S. Pierce, the son of old Benjamin Pierce of Harvard, the great mathematician formerly connected with the coast survey, happened to look into my office. I showed him this manuscript. He was tremendously interested in it, and he took it to a meeting of mathematicians and physicians. Later he wrote a two-column article in the *New York Times* about this manuscript. This attracted a good deal of attention. The manuscript was written at the command of John of Lancaster, duke of Bedford and son of Henry IV. Rollandus dedicates it to him. In this treatise he covers all the theoretical arithmetic known at that time and further treats of irrational numbers, which are now considered a part of algebra.

---

* The John Carter Brown Library at Brown University specializes in early American books. On the occasion of George Arthur Plimpton's lecture on "The Education of Shakespeare" in October of 1924, the eminent president of Brown University, W. H. P. Faunce, wrote: "I still hear the echoes of your excellent lecture in the John Carter Brown Library. A group of the Faculty were discussing it this noon and saying that you were the rare combination, a scholar who has the means to gratify his scholarly tastes."

Pierce advised me not to confine myself to American books but to cover the whole domain of education. Soon after that, on October 10, 1885, I sailed for Europe, armed with a lot of good letters, with the idea of visiting the great public schools together with Oxford and Cambridge Universities. At Cambridge I saw a good deal of J. H. Middleton, who was famous as a historian and who came from one of those old Yorkshire families. He had in his library a good many old schoolbooks that he had inherited. Among them were Henry VIII's primer and Recorde's *Ground of Arts,* the first arithmetic printed in the English language. I had not the slightest idea what to look for in those early books, but he gave me a lot of interesting things to find. From there I went to MacMillan and Bowes, where I bought a chest-full of old books and shipped them back to New York—the greatest find for one to make. They had a secondhand department, and I was fortunate enough to find there a second edition of Recorde's *Ground of Arts,* printed in 1558. The first edition was printed in 1542 and was used at the time Shakespeare was a boy. It had both the Arabic notation and the abacus, which were generally in use in England at that time. This book was in the form of "questions & answer." Recorde realized that in putting arithmetic into the English language he was making a venture, for in the preface he says:

> To please or displease sure I am,
> For not of one sort is every man.
> To please the best sort would I fain,
> The froward displease shall I certayne,
> Yet wish I well (though not with hope)
> All ears and mouths to please or stop.

He emphasized the importance of the study of arithmetic.

It wasn't long after that I found in a bookshop in London the first arithmetic printed in England, by Bishop Tonstall, 1522. He was bishop of Durham. The title page was designed by Holbein.

To the collection of arithmetics I was extremely fortunate to soon add a copy of Pello's arithmetic, which one of the professors at Columbia used to tell his pupils cost as many dollars as there are days in the year. I wanted this because it was the first book using the sign "%" for percent. Others show the first appearance of the signs of equality, plus and minus, etc. Soon afterwards I acquired the first arithmetic printed in Germany—Adam Rieser's arithmetic, wherefore the Germans swear by Rieser as the English do by Cocker.

A manuscript by Benedict has the same old mathematical problems that we have today—the problem of the hogshead, the hare and hound, etc.

A few years ago there were supposed to be only two manuscripts on arithmetic in the English language. Both were in the British Museum. I supposed it would never be possible to secure an English manuscript, but, to my surprise, one was offered for sale in an auction in London, and I gave instructions to purchase it at any price. It is written on vellum, and in addition to treating the different subjects it has quite a number of interesting old poems.

In the meantime I had acquired a good list of the things I wanted, and I had those in mind wherever I went. I remember that on a newsstand in Rome I picked up a first edition of Philipp Callandri's *Arithmetic,* published in 1491, for twenty cents. When I got back to London I saw the same thing for about eight hundred dollars. Not long after this, Brayton Ives's collection of rare books and manuscripts was sold at auction. Among the books was the first arithmetic ever printed—in 1478. It was printed at Treviso, Italy, and sold as a unique copy. When the sale occurred I happened to be in West Virginia and was anxious to get this book. But I was in doubt what to bid. I was not then accustomed to bidding large prices for books. I instructed my partner, Mr. Covant, to go as high as two hundred dollars, which seemed to me a great deal. Later I telegraphed him to go up to $250, and finally, the night before the sale, I told him to go up to $300, and I was very fortunate to get it at that extremely low figure.

Owning now the first arithmetic ever printed, there was nothing for me to do but to purchase all subsequent arithmetics as fast as I could find them. I remember going into Quaritch's bookstore with a list of teachers' and other textbooks, leaving the list and saying I would come in again to see if he had them. I found out he had nearly all of them. Mr. Quaritch himself waited upon me. There were the Lily books, the Whittington and the Stanbridge, the Mulcaster and the Vives. But when I came to ask the price, I found the group would cost me between two and three thousand dollars— more than I was then willing to pay. I remember him asking me if those were the books I wanted. I said that they were. Then he wanted to know why I did not take them. I gave some excuse. He turned and I could see by his manner, when I admitted that I wanted them and didn't take them, that he everlastingly soured on me. A few years afterwards when he found out what I was trying to do and that my means were limited, he was very considerate of me. He said, "Mr. Plimpton, you are one of the best collectors I know. You don't collect because it is a rare book or the only one known. You collect because it fits into your general plan." I have quite a number of books with the compliments of Bernard Quaritch. One gets an advantage in dealing with Quaritch. They usually have what you want and ask a fair price for it.

Once when I was in New Orleans I called at the Howard Library. It was my custom to call at the libraries, because when people had old books they would often inquire at the library what they were worth. I visited the library that had old books but found that they were mostly Italian. But amongst them was a first edition of Roger Ascham's *Schoolmaster*, 1570; Butler's, Howe's, and Ben Jonson's English grammars; and a manuscript of John Hart's *Aegidius Romanus,* the first book printed in English on orthography. Naturally I was anxious to buy those books, but they made the condition that I should take the entire library, which I did not want. I finally made a catalogue of all the Italian books and sent it to Charles Eliot Norton, who taught Italian at Harvard. But he wrote back saying that he did not want them. The Newbury Library had just been established. I sent the list to them, but without success. The result was that I bought the entire collection, thinking I would sell the Italian books. That summer I had the books sent up to my house at Thirty-third Street; Mrs. Plimpton, a graduate of Wellesley College, knew more or less about Italian, and with the help of Quaritch's catalogue we found we had about 125 of the rarest books of the classical period of Italian literature. The library was particularly rich in the romantic or chivalric period in Italian literature. This

Bookplate used to denote items in the collection of rare Italian books presented to Wellesley College by George Arthur Plimpton in memory of his first wife, Frances Taylor Pearsons Plimpton, a graduate of Wellesley

library subsequently became the nucleus that was enlarged until it reached about eleven hundred volumes and was eventually presented to Wellesley College in memory of Mrs. Plimpton. It seems that this collection had originally been made by Richard Henry Wild, the poet who discovered the painting of Dante by Giotto on the walls of the Bargello and who was permitted to remove the plaster with the help of Sir Seymour Kirkop.

Among other things found in the library was a manuscript of Antonio Pucci written in the fourteenth century. This manuscript was included in the library as a gift to Wellesley. The rest of this manuscript was in the Bibliotheca Nazionale in Florence. A facsimile of Wellesley's portion had been sent to that library, and subsequently it was suggested that it might be a good international courtesy, with my consent, to present the original to the Italian library, which thing was done in 1912.

It was along about this time, while I was picking up rare school books, that I started out in earnest to get together the manuscripts and books that were responsible for our present civilization. How did we get where we are? What were the instruments of learning? I took the subject of arithmetic. I had the benefit of DeMorgan's book and also the catalogue of Prince Bon Compagni, and here fortune favored me. I was able to get a tenth-century manuscript of Boethius and another manuscript of Boethius on arithmetic written about 1275. Boethius was called "the last of the Old Romans" and lived about 446. Besides being a great mathematical scholar, he wrote *The Consolation of Philosophy* and suffered martyrdom. At Quaritch's I found the oldest known Latin manuscript of Euclid. It was translated by Campanus from the Arabic manuscript. At that time Campanus was secretary to the Patriarch of Jerusalem, and afterwards he became Pope Urban IV, who was in office from 1261 to 1264. Strange to say, I do not think Quaritch ever knew the value of it, and I only discovered its history through Charles S. Pierce.

Many years ago I bought a collection of manuscripts in Vienna from a catalogue, and amongst these manuscripts was one on algebra, supposedly one of the earliest Latin manuscripts on algebra in the world. A few years ago I was invited by the secretary of the International Mathematical Society— for my library was well known by the mathematicians of Europe—to come and read a paper before their meeting. I accepted, and subsequently the paper was printed in *Science* for October 26, 1928. This paper lists the first arithmetic printed in English, the first one printed in Germany, and the first one printed in America (by Isaac Greenwood, 1728, which I fortunately had secured). Harvard University had a duplicate of this arithmetic, which I secured by trade.

The catalogue of my arithmetics issued by David Eugene Smith shows probably the most complete collection of arithmetics in the world. Without the help of Professor Smith, I doubt very much if I should ever have been able to make this collection. He lists about one hundred manuscripts on arithmetic. The catalogue is entitled *Rara Arithmetica* and was printed in 1908.

My collection involving the subject of reading is quite complete. Many years ago there was sold in London the manuscript of a primer the first page of which contained the series of the letters of the alphabet, the exordium—*Ave Maria*—and the Lord's Prayer. It goes back to the time of Chaucer. It had belonged to Lord Amherst of Hackney. At the auction of his possessions, I was extremely anxious to purchase it as I had regarded it as the foundation of books on the subject of reading. I wrote to Mr. Quaritch asking him to buy it and saying I would place no limit on the price. As we had had a good many dealings together, I knew I could trust him. I was delighted beyond measure when he cabled in that he had purchased it and not at an exorbitant price.

It was many years before I heard of an available hornbook, and when I did hear of one, it was impossible for me to purchase it. In London I called on Andrew Tuer, who was a great authority on hornbooks and had written a book on the subject that contained many facsimiles. I remember seeing in an old paper in Savannah an article that advertised hornbooks, and naturally I searched Georgia hoping I might find one. But I eventually picked them up some in America, some in England, and some in France, so that altogether I have nearly thirty hornbooks. One was offered to me in Guilford, Connecticut, for five hundred dollars. Fortunately, I already had a copy of it. I found one in New Haven for which I paid fifty cents. I found an ivory one for which I paid twenty-five dollars. I have a very early one the first page of which is a hornbook written in silver letters, probably made for the son of some Burgundian duke in France. I am told there are only three books written in silver letters: one Mr. Morgan has, one is in Vienna, and this is the third. I purchased it from John Ruskin's sale. I read a paper once at a meeting of the Antiquarians Society on American hornbooks. My collection is one of the largest in the world.

The following picture, "Tower of Knowledge," is reproduced from the *Margarita Philosophica* written by Gregorius Reisch and printed in 1504. This little picture represents education at that period and shows the teacher, who is to

The "Tower of Knowledge," from the Margarita Philosophica *by Gregorius Reisch, printed in 1504; it illustrates the importance of the hornbook in early sixteenth-century education.*

conduct the boy to the heights of the Tower of Knowledge, handing him a hornbook. The hornbook has upon it the letters of the alphabet, and if the boy masters these letters he will be able to enter the tower. The door through which he must pass is called "Grammar," and the first master under whom he studies is Donatus, who lived in the fourth century and wrote a simple elementary grammar upon the eight parts of speech. Then the student goes up a flight of stairs and studies his large Latin grammar under Priscian, who lived in the sixth century. After the next flight he takes his arithmetic under Boethius, his rhetoric under Cicero, and his logic under

Aristotle; climbing higher he studies astronomy under Ptolemy, geometry under Euclid, and music under Pythagoras, and has now mastered the trivium, or three language studies, and the quadrivium, or four science studies. Finally, he completes his education with moral philosophy under Seneca, natural philosophy under Pliny, and last of all theology under Peter Lombard. Thus you see what an important part the hornbook played in education at the beginning of the sixteenth century—it was the key to unlock all the treasures of learning.

When I first went to England I met a fellow named Shetborough. He had edited a primer, a facsimile of which I have. It was called the *Petit Primer.*

One of the first primers I collected was the *New England Primer.* These primers were the great textbooks from New England that were illustrated and contained the catechism. I reprinted one of mine that had a portrait of General Washington on it. We had given away very many of them on different occasions. Paul Lester Ford of Brooklyn wrote a very interesting book on the *New England Primer,* and since then Charles Heitman of Metuchen, New Jersey, has also written a book on the subject, giving a catalogue of the various editions and telling where they can be found.

It would be impossible to mention all the reading books that followed the *New England Primer.* They sprang up in all sections of this country and were not confined to any one place. In Cincinnati, McGuffey's *Readers* were published. McGuffey was once president of the University of Virginia. His *Readers* ran into a great many editions and had a great influence on the people in the West. In New York State, Sanders' *Readers* were largely used and went to a great many editions. In New England were the Boston, Bingham's, Abner, and Hillyard readers. There were readers for all people: girls' readers, elocutionary, rhetorical, agricultural, political, etc.

I became interested in the English language. How was our language formed? It was made up of Celtic, Roman, the speech of the Anglos and Saxons, Danes and Normans. My library illustrates that formative period, first with an Irish manuscript in Latin, 750. Then with a tenth-century sermon by the Venerable Bede, then a manuscript of Bede's written in 1129 on scientific knowledge, the finding of Easter and the festal days, and what was known of astronomy at that time. I have never been able to get an Anglo-Saxon manuscript. The nearest thing was one of the Anglo-Saxon laws copied in Anglo-Saxon by Roger Ascham in 1556 with his signature. There was an Anglo-Saxon manuscript sold by Lord Lothian in New York in 1933, but it brought fifty-five thousand dollars.

I have a very interesting Danish manuscript. The Danes occupied England from 1013 to 1033, and the Normans came in 1066. To illustrate that period I have manuscripts in Latin and Norman French. French continued to be the language of the courts and the nobility until 1366, when English took its place. The struggle from that day on was between English and Latin. The earliest English manuscripts I have are:

- Richard Rolle, the mystic, who became a friar. I have his *Pricke of Conscious,* about 1300.
- Walter Hylton
- The Brut manuscript
- The *Chronicles of England*
- Two manuscripts of John Wycliffe, the New Testament and the Bible, and a sermon
- Chaucer: four pages of "The Franklyn's Tale," and the only perfect manuscript of "The Astrolabe," manuscript on astrology and witchcraft
- John Gower's *Confessio Amantis,* 1400
- William of Malmesbury's *Life of William the Conqueror,* about 1150
- John Lydgate, *Fall of the Princes* and *The Court of Sapience*
- The *Compendium of Knowledge* of Bartholomus Anglicus. Bartholomus lived in Paris about 1250. My manuscript is probably the third largest in the world, according to the librarian of the Vatican.
- I have also several thousand English grammars.

The finding in New Orleans of the first edition of Ben Jonson's, Howe's, and Butler's grammars and the first book on orthography by John Hart gave me a real zest for the subject. W. H. Wells, who was the principal of one of the Chicago schools, many years ago got interested in the subject of English. He was the author of several grammars. He made a collection—the best collection up to that time. He died and the collection was put on the market, but nobody wanted it. In due time I purchased it. Although it contained many duplicates of what I had, still his and my collections together made one of the best collections of English grammars in the country.

Lindly Murray was a native of Lancaster and a Quaker. His English grammars were widely used not only in this country, but also in England. My library has a first edition of each one. It has also a first edition of each of Noah Webster's three books and a first edition of Gould Brown's grammar and of Greene's *English Grammar.* Altogether there must be between three and four thousand grammars. My library is also rich in books on the development of character. These are sometimes in the form of reading books or books on the subject of good manners. "Manners maketh the man" was an important subject in many of these early books.

Closely identified with books on grammar are spelling books. I remember being in Oxford, England, and one of the people connected with the Bodleian Library, in speaking of spelling books, said he had a letter from a London dealer telling of a spelling book printed in Oxford, but the authorities hesitated to purchase it on account of the price. I said, "Yes, I saw it. The dealer offered it to me and I bought it for my collection of spelling books." He said, "That's the way of the world. Unless we purchase these old books as soon as they turn up, we lose them."

I have tried to get only American geographies. I felt that making a European collection of them with old maps was hardly worthwhile in view of the large collections that were already in this country. But I do have a twelfth-century manuscript of Isidore of Seville. In the manuscript is a map of the world as it was known at that time. Subsequently, I bought the first printed edition of Isidore's *Etymologies,* printed in 1469, and there I found the map printed. This is undoubtedly the first map of the world ever printed.

The type of books in which I was extremely interested were the Latin texts. Latin was the backbone, you might say, of education from the very beginning. The first Latin grammar was written by Donatus, who lived in the fourth century and wrote a very elementary Latin grammar. He was the teacher of Saint Jerome, and his little Latin grammar was in constant use, probably, for over a thousand years. I was fortunate very early in collecting class-books to secure two or three manuscripts of Donatus, and better still, a first edition of the author.

The first book that Gutenberg printed was not the Bible, as is generally supposed, but a Donatus. There were supposed to be two specimens of this; one happens to be a leaf in the British Museum, and I also have a leaf. The type is the same as that of the Bible. It is always difficult to say that one has the only perfect specimen, for I have purchased many books that were reported to me as such, and subsequently I found other editions.

The next great grammar was Priscian, and I have a beautiful illuminated manuscript of this author. This is the grammar that mentions a great many authors whose works do not now exist. Scholars are constantly hoping that some of these authors may turn up. Among the rare items in this list of Latin grammars is Lily's Latin grammar printed in 1512 or 1513 in a first edition. This also appeared in subsequent editions and was used almost up to the beginning of the last century, when it was only with the greatest difficulty that Parliament permitted other Latin grammars to be used in England.

A very interesting article was written by Professor George Lyman Kittridge on the Latin grammars in my library. It describes not only the first English, French, German, and Italian editions, but also the first to be used in the United States.

Supplementing the Latin grammars is a large collection of the classical Latin authors. I have the manuscripts of Caesar, Virgil's *Eclogues* and *Georgics*, Terence, Cornelius Nepos, and Cicero's *De Senectute* and *De Rhetorica.* In fact, I possess most of the classics: Seneca, Horace, Juvenal, etc. In addition to the manuscripts are the printed editions of the classical authors. There are interesting stories connected with getting this library together. For instance, the manuscript of

Caesar was presented to me by James Loeb, who started the series of classical authors and is now living in Munich. A great many items in this collection came from Joseph Martini, who formerly had a shop here in New York but is now located in Lugano, Switzerland. I owe probably more to him than to any other person in calling my attention to these manuscripts and books. I remember when he first came to New York, a stranger, without friends and scarcely understanding the English language. He has been more or less my constant companion and helper in forming my library.

I have one of the first printed editions of Virgil, printed by Aldus and formerly owned by Philipp Melanchthon. I have also a Juvenal that formerly belonged to Sir Isaac Newton and was used by him when a student at Trinity College, Cambridge.

In Greek and Latin, my library has two manuscripts on Greek grammar. It has also the first Greek dictionary, printed in 1478. Among the early printed editions of the Greek grammars are Gaza and Lascaris. One contains the autograph of the first professor of Greek at Oxford University. Among the texts is a very interesting lectionary bible of the tenth century, and also a great many single leaves of the Greek writers. It has the complete manuscripts of Homer's *Iliad* and *Odyssey* said to have belonged to Ariosto and containing notes in his handwriting and his autograph. I have the first Aldine edition of Homer that formerly belonged to Philipp Melanchthon, with all his notes in his own handwriting. On the title page he writes, "The reverend father Martinus Luther, theologue from Philipp Melanchthon." Some of the notes are in the handwriting of Luther, but most are in Melanchthon's hand. In the *Iliad* he writes the same as he did in the *Odyssey*, but in Greek instead of Latin. I have the first printed edition of Melanchthon's Greek grammar, and the notes in this are all in the handwriting of Melanchthon. I remember when the Melanchthon and Erasmus books were put up at auction in London. They had formerly belonged to Hodgkin, a Quaker, who had written a history of Rome. I was present at the auction, and by arrangement with the dealer, if the price went beyond my means, I was to raise my hat and the bidding would stop. When the Virgil was put up, I purchased it and also the manuscripts of Erasmus. When it came to the books that Melanchthon had given to Martin Luther, the price kept going up, up, up, until finally, much to my regret, I had to take my hat off. Afterwards, when I went to see what man had gotten it, I found it was Mr. Quaritch, who said, "Mr. Plimpton, I bought this Melanchthon for a man in Tangiers, Africa. If I had known that you wanted it, I would have seen to it that you got it." I requested that if this man, whose name was Farris, did not want it, please to see that I got it. Two weeks later, a representative came to me and said, "Mr. Plimpton, you have the first chance at this, and may buy it if you wish." I did so, and the books are invaluable in a library that illustrates the history of education.

First Journey to England

Friday night, with my brother Edward, I secured big state-room No. 3 in the stern of the steamer *Gallia,* Cunard Line. Made all the preparations for the start at 7:00 Saturday morning.

After a good night's rest we rose at 5:30 and reached our steamer at 6:30. Dr. Northrup came to see me off and introduced me to Mr. Leonard, who was to be my ship companion.

At 7:00 A.M. sharp, all went ashore and bid goodbye to Edward and Dr. Northrup. As soon as we were fairly started and as we were swinging out into the river, I wrote some letters to be sent by the pilot. Soon after, we were assigned our breakfast. Mr. Leonard, myself, and several others at the Doctor's table. Among these was Mr. Hammill, a Colorado coal miner and ranch owner, a wealthy man and quite a talker. He is to attend a stockholders meeting of his mining companies in London. Mr. Kolleck of Boston, a teller in a bank, on a vacation. Colonel Evers, the largest land owner in America, who claims to own, in his own name, one million acres in Mississippi. He is a great talker and believer in England. He is on his return to London. A Mr. Benedict of the Remington Typewriter. He goes to place his machine upon the English market. Also a gentleman from Australia on a visit to America. Mrs. McGee, two daughters—very pretty—and son and cousin. These with the Doctor make up our table, and a very pleasant table it is.

I enjoyed my breakfast, and when we got through we were fairly out to sea, bound for England. It has taken me a long time to realize that I am going to England. I have had the idea so long in my mind that even now I can hardly realize that the next land I shall see will be Ireland. Saturday's sail was delightful, and everybody was well and the sea was smooth. I sat in my chair with my rug on my knees all day.

Retired Saturday night at 10:00. I slept well. Sunday was a repetition of Saturday, no swell and very pleasant weather. We made from Saturday noon to Sunday noon 335 miles and about 45 miles from 7:00 A.M. to noon Sunday.

We had the English Service read by the first officer, and after the Service, Mr. Pettes, a London cracker manufacturer—so he informed me—spoke. He took as his text, "Words fitly spoken are like golden apples set in pictures of silver." He belongs, so he told me, to the Plymouth Brethren. All members of this body take the Bible as their guide and all can explain and preach it.

Sunday night the steamer began to roll and pitch, and as the wind was with us, all the sails were set.

Monday, strong northwestern winds. We made 349 miles.

Tuesday, wind increasing and heavy rolling of the boat.

Wednesday, we made 319 miles and are now in the midst of a storm with very heavy seas. The steamer takes in water on both sides and one can hardly keep in a chair. Nearly all of the passengers have been sick. I myself have been uneasy but have not thrown up. I feel all the time as though I should do so and believe it would be good for me to do so. I never before realized what it was to cross the ocean. On all previous land journeys, should I care to give up the trip, I could do so; but no matter how unpleasant this trip is there is no other way than to bear it. Sometimes it seems as though I could not bear it longer, and yet my condition has been rather pleasant when compared to others'. I have been at the table every meal and have been on deck all the time, while many others are unable to be out of their staterooms.

During the rest of the voyage the ship continued to roll until about two days before we reached Fastnet Lighthouse. Then the steamer began to pitch; this was a new sensation, but as I had got used to the sea I did not mind it. It was great to watch the ship ride upon the great waves and then to see it plunge into the trough and put its bow under some great waves. Some of the passengers who could be well during the rolling of the ship became sick at the pitching.

Saturday night we had a concert in aid of the Sailors Orphan Asylum in Liverpool. It was made up of concerts, recitations, music, etc. About fifteen pounds was raised. Sunday we had the English Service and Mr. Pettes again talked. During the evening I listened to him talk to the steerage passengers. At about 10:00 P.M. we saw the Fastnet Light. Our ship burned colored lights and sent up colored rockets in order that the keeper of the lighthouse might know the name of our steamer. At 2:30 Monday morning we were at Queenstown. I gave a telegram to the purser to be sent to John, my oldest brother, informing him of my arrival. The telegram was like a letter and required 12d stamps. All day Monday we sailed up through the English Channel and Irish Sea. The Welsh Mountains in the east could be seen, and when we reached Holyhead it seemed as though we were near England. At about 7:30 P.M. we were in the Mercer River and soon after in the dock, and suspecting that John was on a tender lying alongside I called him by name and was pleased to hear his voice and soon after to meet not only him, but Carrie, his wife. I felt quite honored to see them both. Soon afterwards we were at the custom house and our baggage was passed and we were on the boat to Egremont. Was much pleased with John's home. It is a very pleasant home—furnished in most excellent taste. What pleased me the most was to see their son, J.C.P., Jr., who was born some five months ago. This is the first Plimpton boy of the second generation, and by all indications he will do credit to his name. After much exchange of news we all retired.

During Tuesday and Wednesday I became familiar with John's business and was agreeably surprised at its magnitude, and more so by its history. Seven years ago he landed in Liverpool, a stranger without money, without friends, and nothing but a few samples, but with plenty of pluck, perseverance, and ability—to do hard work. His success against such odds is marvelous, and I think we all have reason to feel proud of him. Each year his business has grown, and three times he has been obliged to move to larger quarters. What capital he has had, he has made. At present he has recently purchased one-half interest in a horseshoe nail manufactory, to be called the Plimpton Horse Shoe Nail Company. The outlook here seems good, and I shall be much disappointed if he does not make considerable money.

Wednesday night I spent on the way to Dublin. We went by way of Holyhead. The boat has a first class and second class. We went first class and upon arrival of the train rushed to secure our berths. There are no staterooms but easy lounges—first comes helps himself. We were fortunate enough to secure two good ones, and wrapping ourselves up in our blankets were soon asleep. The boats furnish no coverings, and hence one must carry his own.

At 7:30 we reached Dublin. After a short railroad ride we were soon upon a jaunting car. One sits over the wheel on each side. This one would carry four persons besides the driver. By means of its two wheels, one can get over the ground fastly. After our breakfast I visited Trinity College. I was unable for some time to meet any of the professors but at last met Professor Palmer (Latin). He seemed very glad to meet me and explained to me the object of the different buildings. With him I visited the dining hall where the students take their meals at 6:00 P.M. A table is set aside for the fellows. The library contains 260,000 volumes. He invited me to lunch with him, and I met Professors Tyrell and Mahaffy. The lunch was served in his study. An old Irish woman attended upon us, but she was little help. The most she did was to bring in the food, and then we all helped ourselves. Spent two very pleasant hours with them. College has 1,200 students and about 250 received degrees last year. The course in the college is similar to ours. Much attention is paid to the ancient languages. Hope to visit Dublin and examine their methods more thoroughly.

Visited Dublin Castle, Royal College of Ireland, Wesley College. In this last college the students all sleep in one large room. I counted fifty beds in one room.

Visited Liverpool College. Saw E. C. Selwyn, President. They begin Latin with Ritchie's *First Steps in Latin,* Allen's *Latin Grammar* and *Latin Lessons.* Age of pupils about nine years. Pupils prepared for Oxford and Cambridge examinations. Pronunciation of Latin, Roman. Teaching of Greek same as Latin.

Oxford. I arrived at this place Tuesday night at 7:30 and found at the Mitre Hotel a note from Mr. Underhill, whom I met in New York two years ago, wishing me to stop at Magdalen College with him. I sent word that I could not do it the first night but should be glad to do so during the rest of my stay. Mitre Hotel is about five hundred years old, and a very quaint building it is. As far as possible they tried to keep the house upon the old plan, just as little change as possible has been made in the building. The entrance is large enough for carriages. On the side of the entrance hangs meat of all kinds. The office is made up of a collection of a little of everything, such as bar room, drawers for the bread, drawers for the silver, a place where china is displayed. The clerks are ladies, and they deal out liquor to all comers. The floors are all tiled with stone, and a large open fireplace displays the red hot coals. A lady clerk showed me my room, which is furnished, as I was told, as near like it was four hundred years ago as they could get. In the morning a pail full of hot water was brought without my order and placed in a foot-bath tub.

The next day I presented my letter to Mr. Matherson, fellow of New College. He at once invited me to dine with him at 6:30. At noon I moved my baggage into New Building of Magdalen College, into a room of a student (or commoner, as he is called) who had been rusticated. The room is 150 years old and is furnished elegantly. It is heated by an open fire and lighted by candles.

I took lunch at 1:00 P.M. with Mr. Underhill in what is known as the Commoner's Room. This is an immense room at least four hundred years old, furnished elegantly. I met here the president of the college and the fellows. They all lunched together.

On November 28, 1885, at 1:00 P.M., I was at the landing stage in Liverpool with my baggage, which consisted of thirteen packages all marked for the *Aurania* bound for New York. John and Carrie came to the stage and went with me on the tender to the *Aurania*. A strong west wind was blowing. We soon reached the steamer and they saw me settled in room 79. I bid them goodbye and felt very sorry to leave them. They have both been very kind to me and made my visit to England very pleasant. They were the first to greet me and the last to bid me goodbye. I wish I might have brought them with me. We three should have had a very pleasant time.

Through John's friend, Mr. Hitchcock, I became acquainted with Mr. Stevens, a recent graduate of Yale College who has been spending four months sight-seeing in Europe. I find a lot of pleasant people to look at and hope that upon their acquaintance I shall like them.

Our first night in the Irish Channel, owing to the storm, our ship rolled a great deal, so much so that I did not sleep. In the morning at 7:00 we were at Queenstown. It is a beautiful harbor. I was much amused to see the little Irish rowboats alongside, their owners selling apples, etc., to the steerage passengers. The wind was very strong and they ran great risk in their venture. When the tender from the shore came alongside, I went ashore. There I was besieged by beggars, peddlers of shamrock, shillalahs, black thorn sticks, etc. Each one gave me some shamrock and their blessing, and then if I did not pay them a penny, they cursed me. Soon the mail train arrived, and after the bags were put aboard, we were soon off to the steamer. I was much pleased with Queenstown. It is beautifully located and its harbor must be one of the finest in the world. While on shore I met Mr. Drummond of Dublin. He had just seen a Miss Christiansen on board and asked me to introduce myself to her, as she had no friends. Such opportunities I always avail myself of, especially when the young lady is good-looking.

At 1:30 P.M. we started for the Atlantic in the face of a strong westerly wind blowing almost a gale. As soon as we got into the ocean the ship rolled and pitched a great deal. I began to feel shaky. I went to dinner at 6:00 P.M. but did not enjoy it owing to the pitching. Retired at 10:00 P.M.

Monday morning got up at 8:30 after a bad night's sleep. All during this day the ship continued to toss about. Had no appetite. Did not go to lunch but did go to dinner. Had no sooner got away from dinner than I threw it up for the fishes.

Tuesday did not feel any better. A strong westerly wind had been blowing all the morning, and from 1:00 to 4:00 P.M. it blew a real gale. It was a grand sight to see the sea. It was thoroughly maddened. The foam and high waves were almost great hills following close upon each other. The ship shook as each struck her. At about 3:00 the sail (foresail) gave way and there was great excitement. The ship rolled so that much water was taken in. The gale only lasted about two hours, but the rolling was very bad.

Wednesday did not sleep well. Could hardly stay in my berth. During the day it rained hard.

Thursday it rained all day.

Friday we are off the bank of Newfoundland and it is very cold.

Have made very many acquaintances—among our passengers is General Wallace, author of *Ben Hur.*

Second Journey
to England

On Friday, March 2nd, I determined to sail for England on the following morning on the *Umbria* at 9:30 A.M. The object of the trip was to make arrangements for the sale of our publications in England. It had been determined for some time that I should go, but the date of departure was not fixed until the day before sailing. Through my friend, W. H. Stanford, I secured not simply a good stateroom at less than the usual price, but also a letter of introduction to President Robinson and family, who were to be my ship companions. After making all arrangements, such as looking after my business and the details of sailing, I was at the dock at 9:00 A.M. My sister Priscilla, Miss Wilson, my brother Edward, Mr. Hall, Mr. Cutter and wife, Mr. Conant, and Mr. Sayler were there to bid me goodbye. We started promptly at 9:30, and as we moved out into the stream I felt a sort of relief come over me. I had not realized until then that for at least one week I should be relieved of all business cares and could rest and sleep as much as I desired. I have been constantly at work for two years without any change, and while I feel well and could attend to the business, yet I do not have the enthusiasm one ought to have. This I believe the trip will return to me.

We made the first day about 459 miles; the weather was very pleasant, but the ship began to roll. Most of the ladies began to grow sick. Our second day's run was 440 miles.

Our third day's run 428 miles.

Our fourth day's run 444 miles.

Our fifth day's run 435 miles.

Our sixth day's run 435 miles.

Our seventh day's run 225 miles.

We reached Fastnet Light about 9:00 on Friday night. This is considered a very fast voyage, and while not the fastest yet, it lacked only a few hours of being so.

All day Thursday we had a very rough day, a regular

gale blowing and a very rough sea. The constant rolling of the ship was marked throughout the whole voyage. I find I have been to every meal but yet I have not enjoyed a single meal since we left Sandy Hook. While a majority of the passengers have been sick more or less, I find that I have not felt well and would gladly have paid my tribute, yet I could not do it. We have been fortunate in having a table where there are some good fellows who have been at the tables constantly. Mr. Perie, a Scotchman from Aberdeen, Mr. Corbett, a barrister from London, Mr. Stratton, of Jones, McDurfee & Stratton of Boston, Mr. Warning from Pittsburgh, whom I had known before, Mr. Benjamin from New York, and a Mr. Manville from London. We had a very pleasant party. I shall doubtless see these men again. Among us passengers we had the Right Honorable Joseph Chamberlain, who is on his return to England from the Fisheries Commission, Phil Armour and family from Chicago, and Mr. Dufree and family from Boston, who are sort of cousins. At this point of writing we are in the Irish Channel, and it looks as though we should reach Liverpool this evening.

I found at my table a letter from my brother John in Liverpool, stating that he was glad I was coming. He told me that my brother Herbert reached New York last Sunday on the *Aurania* from Liverpool. I was anxious to postpone the day of my sailing until he reached home, but as it was important for me to reach London as soon as possible, I concluded it best to sail without seeing him. He had been gone some three months. I am very glad that this trip is so nearly ended. While I am conscious of feeling much better and while I believe the trip has benefited me very much, I am not one of those who are very happy on the sea. This morning I have been all over the machinery and the fire rooms of the steamer. Their magnitude is something wonderful. There are seventy-two fires and they consume 350 tons of American coal and 320 of English coal per day. For the courtesy of seeing the ship I am indebted to Mr. Robertson, who has two brothers in my brother's store in England.

I think I will go up on deck and watch the Irish and Welsh coast.

Francis with Merrylegs

As Francis's mother died when he was born, George Arthur Plimpton was left to bring up their little son alone. He was helped in the beginning by his mother-in-law, Mrs. Sarah Taylor Pearsons, who came to live at 61 Park Avenue. He must have used the executive talents that had taken him to the top of Ginn & Company to handle his household. He found excellent women to care for the boy—first a Miss Leonard, a nurse, for his younger years, and then a governess, Miss Cook, of whom Francis was very fond.

George Arthur Plimpton kept in very close touch with Francis, writing to him when they were separated and expecting a letter every week, even when Francis was in college.

Some of George Arthur Plimpton's letters to Francis have survived. He dictated the early letters—when Francis was six and seven—from his New York office, pasting in pictures of interest. Then there follows a series of letters handwritten while he was on a trip to Alaska, when Francis was ten. The letters, which are not in the least condescending, describe events of the time and George Arthur Plimpton's own thoughts on the state of the world.

EDWIN GINN

G. A. PLIMPTON   FRED B. GINN
LEWIS PARKHURST   O. P. CONANT
T. W. GILSON   F. M. AMBROSE
H. H. HILTON   RICHARD S. THOMAS
     C. H. THURBER

Ginn & Company, Publishers

OF

SCHOOL AND COLLEGE TEXT-BOOKS.

BOSTON. NEW YORK. CHICAGO. LONDON.

Dictated by

70 Fifth Ave., New York,   January 25, 1906.

My dear Francis:-

     Your grandmother writes me that you have been off on a visit.
You will have to tell me all about it when I get there next Saturday.

     What do you think of a train of cars like this?.

THE CHILDREN'S TRAIN

I think I should not care to travel that
way. I should rather travel on the train
of cars that Grandmother travels on; or
in fact, better than that I should rather
ride on an elephant the same as these people
are doing. Sometime you and I will have
to take a ride on an elephant.

81

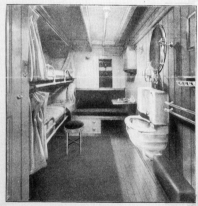

FIRST CABIN STATEROOM

How would you like to be in one of
these boats? This is the stateroom you would have. You would
have to sleep in one of these little bunks.

Here is a chart showing the way
they would sail. They follow the
red lines, along the coast. You
get your globe and find New York
and then find New Orleans. Then
follow along these read lines around
Florida. You will see the lighthouses all along the shore where the
stars are. If it wasn't for these lighthouses, the sailors out at sea
wouldn't know where they were.

Affectionately yours, Geo. A. Plimpton

82

EDWIN GINN
G. A. PLIMPTON   FRED B. GINN
LEWIS PARKHURST   O. P. CONANT
T. W. GILSON   F. M. AMBROSE
H. H. HILTON   RICHARD S. THOMAS
          C. H. THURBER

Ginn & Company, Publishers

OF

SCHOOL AND COLLEGE TEXT-BOOKS.

BOSTON. NEW YORK. CHICAGO. LONDON.

Dictated by   *70 Fifth Ave., New York*, March 2, 1906.

Dear Francis:-

　　When the people first came to this country, there were no
houses for them to live in; so the first thing they had to do was to
put up a house.　Now, here
is a picture of the kind of
house they used to build down
South.　Then, after they
had lived in this　for a while
they would tear it down and
build a frame house.　They
found the Indians living in
tents.　This is a tent some-

thing like what the Indians had, but it is the tent of some campers.
You see they have shot a bear and have skinned it and put the skin up
on the side of the tent.
Another hunter has just
come in with another great
big bear.

　　Now, this is
the sort of train that I
came home on.　It is
the mile-a-minute train.

83

Ginn & Company, Publishers

When I was in Kentucky, they wanted me to go down in the great Mammoth Cave, but I didn't care to go.   The picture shows some people in a boat in the cave.   They have to have it lighted.

Affectionately your father,

Geo. A. Plimpton
H.

Dec. 4, 1906.

My dear Francis:–

To-morrow you will be six years old, and you don't know how sorry I am that I can't be with you. When I was six years old, I lived at the old homestead, and I used to go to school down at the first house as you go towards the station. We had little benches to sit on and we had a private teacher. My birthday came on the 13th of July. Your uncle Edward was about five years old and your uncle Herbert, about three years old.

At that time there was a great deal of excitement throughout the whole country. Fort Sumter had been fired upon and President Lincoln was calling for soldiers to put down the Rebellion. All the boys wanted to be soldiers. I remember I wanted to be a soldier; I wanted to go to the war as a drummer boy. The boys would all form themselves into little companies and we would take sticks and pretend we were soldiers. I remember going with my father a few years after this down to the camp at Readville. There were a lot of soldiers there. A good many of my father's workmen were there, and he took down pies and cake to give to them; and I remember how this little visit made me want to be a soldier. I didn't know in those days what it was to be a soldier, how many of them would lose their lives; but the time is coming, I hope, when we shall have no more wars. When people and nations get angry with each other, they will not fight, but will settle all their troubles by arbitration.

The old house was not the one that is there now; it had four Doric columns in front of it.

I took dinner last Sunday with Horatio Hathaway Brewster, and he was six years old last week. He is just one week older than you are. He wanted to know all about you, and I told him you would come and see him very soon.

Now, I shall be home Sunday morning, and I have got a birthday present for you. I don't think you can guess what it will be, but I am sure it will please you. Give Grandmother a good kiss and tell her she must kiss you six times for me, and with best wishes to Miss Leonard, I am

Your affectionate father,
Geo. A. Plimpton

Master Francis T. P. Plimpton,
Lewis Farm,
Walpole, Mass.

January 4, 1907.

Dear Francis:

You think it is great fun to have a ride on the choo-choo cars, but I think it would be more fun to ride on a camel, and suppose we take a ride sometime. Here is the camel, you see, all ready, loaded with his trunk, his baskets and his tent. He is all ready for the march.

s Stereograph, Copyrighted 1900, by H. C. White Co., N. Y.

READY FOR THE MARCH.

Then, we would ride until the middle of the day, and when the middle of the day came, we would pitch our tent and sit under it, and rest and get cool.

y H. C. White Co., N. Y.

HALT FOR A LITTLE REST.

CAMPING OUT.

Then, at night we would camp out and somebody would tell us stories. You
see them all seated around here listening to stories. When you are a little older, I think you and I will have to take such a trip.

EUROPEAN TRAVELERS IN THE DESERT AND
THEIR GUIDES.

Here are some people
who have been out to
the Pyramids in Egypt,
and here they are
right by the Sphinx.

A DEVOTEE'S RETREAT FOR PRAYER AND MEDITATION.

Here is a man making his prayer right in the middle of the day.
You see he has taken off his shoes and he faces toward Mecca, and I should
think the old camel was praying, too.   He is evidently a pretty good man,
for you see how fat the camel is, and he has a good face, too.

Your affectionate father,

Geo. A. Plimpton

Ginn & Company, Publishers

OF

SCHOOL AND COLLEGE TEXT-BOOKS

BOSTON NEW YORK CHICAGO LONDON

EDWIN GINN
G. A. PLIMPTON   FRED B. GINN
LEWIS PARKHURST   O. P. CONANT
T. W. GILSON   F. M. AMBROSE
H. H. HILTON   RICHARD S. THOMAS
C. H. THURBER   T. B. LAWLER

Dictated by G. A. P.

70 Fifth Avenue, New York, August 14, 1907.

Dear Francis:

Suppose you were walking along through the woods just as this little girl is and should meet two just such looking people. What would you do? Aren't you surprised that the little girl isn't running away? They must be brothers; I should think very likely twins, shouldn't you? They must be very fond of each other, because you see they have their arms around each others necks. Notice the big umbrella. I guess they must live in a country where it rains a good deal, although I should think in the woods they would not need an umbrella.

From the way they look, I should think they were accustomed to take whatever food is set before them. Shouldn't you? Whether it is wheatena, or barley, or cracked wheat, or oatmeal, or eggs, or hash. What do you think the little girl is thinking of when she first sees them? And evidently they don't know what to make of the little girl. You find out all about it and let me know what you think of it. I will bring home a book some day that will tell you all about it, but in the meantime you think about it and when you read the book you will know who these people are.

How is the pony?   Give him plenty of exercise.   Give my love
to your Grandmother and Cousin Ruby and your Aunt Edith.

Affectionately,

Geo. A. Plimpton

Master Francis T. P. Plimpton.

Dec. 6, 1907.

Dear Francis:

To-morrow you will be seven years old, and I am afraid I shall not be with you to help you celebrate the day.

When I was seven years old, I lived at the old homestead, but in a different kind of a house. You will find a picture of it in the guest chamber at the old homestead. There are four Doric columns in front of the house.

At that time there was a great war going on between the North and the South, and I remember going with my father in a carriage that was filled chuck full with pies and cakes and apples and other things for the soldiers at Readville, where they were camped out and were being trained so that they would be able to do good service in the war that was going on. I remember, too, when Uncle David and Uncle Jason came home from the war with their soldier clothes on, how anxious I was to go back with them as a drummer boy; but of course I was too young.

This was the year when the little Monitor sailed out of New York harbor and went down along the Jersey coast to Fortress Monroe. When the people saw it coming they said, "There comes a Yankee cheese-box." But it came just in time, for the Merrimac had destroyed most of the ships, and there were only two or three more to destroy, and then they were planning to sail up to New York or somewhere else. I remember as a boy how happy everybody was when the news came that this little cheese-box, the Monitor, had destroyed the Merrimac.

It was not a great while after this that Admiral Farragut went up the Mississippi River. New Orleans was defended by strong forts and the Confederates had put old hulks in the river to stop him, but this did not prevent Farragut from going up the river.

Then, just a little later, President Lincoln issued his Emancipation Proclamation, in which he freed all the negroes and forever abolished slavery in this country. So you see that when I was seven years old, there were stirring times. Now everything is peaceful. There are no wars going on anywhere in the world at this time, and we ought all of us to be very thankful.

I hope you are staying out doors all you can. There is nothing like fresh air.

I am going to bring to you when I come a copy of Robinson Crusoe illustrated, and I gave Grandmother for you a little book on riddles. I have not been able yet to get you a submarine boat. Here is something that will get you ten cents.

Remember me kindly to Grandmother and tell her to give you seven good kisses for me; and also remember me to Miss Leonard.

Affectionately your father,
Geo. A. Plimpton

Master Francis T. P. Plimpton.

Francis with workhorses at the Lewis Farm

**On board special train for Seattle and Alaska
June 18, 1910**

My dear Francis:

This has been an eventful day. President Roosevelt after a year and quarter in Africa and Europe is back and passed by the office at 1:00 today. He stood in the carriage and waved his hat to the delighted people. It was a great ovation and one that must have pleased him very much. He had in his escort the rough riders and the Spanish war veterans. The two Abenethey boys, one nine years and the other six years, who rode all the way from Oklahoma, attracted a great deal of attention. It was a great sight and I wished you could have seen it.

Here I am at 10:20, just five hours from Jersey City on this special train. The host and hostess are Jacob H. Schiff and wife. The banker and head of the firm of Kuhn Loeb and Company and the guests are Professor and Mrs. Loeb, Miss Wise, General James Harrison Wilson, Mr. Edgar Saliu—Mr. Schiff's nephew from Frankfort—and one of his nephews by the name of Manfred Schiff. Mr. Sulzberger, who goes only to Chicago, and your father. Nine in all. Our train consists of a baggage car, a pullman state room car, a combination car, that is a kitchen, dining room, four big staterooms, and an observation room. All this is for nine people. At 5:30 we all sat around a table and had tea. Mrs. Schiff pouring it. At 7:30 we all sat down to a regular dinner and it seemed like a family dinner. We had celery soup, fish, chicken, green corn, string beans, potatoes, rice and fruit compote, lettuce and tomato salad, ice cream, cheese, and coffee. After dinner Mr. Schiff offered up his thanks and then every one said *mae zish* and shook hands with each other; one could not but be impressed with the beautiful spirit that seemed to dominate all present. Some twenty or more books have been purchased for our enjoyment, and someone sent Mrs. Schiff ten pounds of candy, which she shared with us all. My stateroom is in the middle car and center of it, and it seems to have everything except the bathroom. Everybody seems to have retired so I guess I will.

Sunday, June 19. I awoke at 5:00 A.M. and looked out of

the window on Pittsburgh and the great iron works. We followed the Ohio River for some distance and on each side there were great works. Saw several steamers with the paddle wheels behind the boats. The Pressed Car Steel Works, American Bridge Works, etc. There was so much smoke and fog that the sun had great difficulty in making itself known. We are now in Ohio and it would do Mr. Wilson* good to see so much rich land without any stones. I should not want him to see it, if it would make him want to leave the Lewis Farm. Someday we will make the Lewis Farm much better than it is now.

We have just come from breakfast. All kinds of fruit, eggs, liver and bacon, buckwheat cakes and coffee. We all put our watches back one hour. What was 7:00 in New York is 6:00 here and when we get farther west we shall have to change again. It is now 10:00 and with you it is 11:00 and you are in church. I wish I could be there with you. My church attendance will have to be on the train.

Professor Loeb tells me that he was born in Ohio and is a brother of Mrs. Schiff. He was professor of Chemistry in the University of the City of New York but resigned a few years ago and devotes his time to study and original investigation. He is very well informed and a most interesting man to talk with. His wife, who is with him, is very pleasant. They have two children. Mrs. Schiff said she wanted to take her grandson, who is twelve-and-a-half years old, and if she had taken him she would have asked you to come. One boy she thought would have had a lonesome time. I have bought a new camera and can take some pictures, which I hope will give you some idea of the trip.

Mr. Sulzberger, who owns Schwarzschild and Sulzberger Company, stops at Chicago. He tells me he has eight sons and four daughters. He is a butcher and sells $100,000,000 worth of meat a year. His is the third largest packing house in the world. *Armour first, Swift second, and his third.* He has large butcher shops on the East River near Forty-seventh Street. He sends cattle (live) to Europe and said anytime I wanted a

---

* The manager of the Lewis Farm in Walpole.

free passage for a friend, he would give it to him provided he would tend cattle on the way over. I have known quite a number of boys who have been to Europe this way. He built this business up by first being a good man. People said that they could always depend upon him, that he kept his promises. Second because he knew his business. He knew all about it. This took time, patience, and perseverance, and he was able to teach others after a while so that they could do it for him. He told me that he would show me how to can my hams and treat the pigs when they are killed at the Lewis Farm.

Tell Mr. Wilson that here in Ohio I passed great fields of clover a foot high. That the fields are plowed under to enrich the soil. They do this when they have no manure. Hope to hear from you at Seattle.

Your affectionate father,
Geo. A. Plimpton

Nebraska near Wyoming
June 20, 1910

My dear Francis:

It is Sunday night and we are in the great state of Iowa, the home of the Dollivers. I think the country west of Chicago and in this state the finest I have ever seen. The soil is so fertile and the growing grains look very well. The cattle and sheep are literally in clover. I wonder what our cows would think of such feed. As we made no stop in Chicago I did not see Aunt Carrie or Mr. Stelton as I had telegraphed them I would. I presume they were not at the station to meet me.

Monday morning we arrived at Omaha, and now we are in Nebraska. As far as you can see the land is level giant fields of wheat, oats, corn, and cattle. We are now on the Union Pacific Railroad, and Mr. Schiff says this is his 'road. In 1897 he and several others bought the 'road at bankrupt sale. At that time the 'road was in a bad way. Its stock was selling at $5 per share. Now it is selling at $175. It has been up to $200

96

per share. The vice president of the 'road is now with us. He tells me that this land is worth $100 to $150 per acre. A few years ago these people purchased it from the government for $1.50 per acre. The country now looks very prosperous. Our train is going at the rate of fifty miles an hour. The vice president says that if the corn is knee high by July Fourth it means that they will have a very large crop. It is now six inches.

Edgar Saliu, a German boy eighteen years old, a nephew of Mr. Schiff who lives at Frankfort and is a student at Heidelberg University, is with us. He came especially to take this trip and landed only a few days ago. He tells me he began French when he was nine, Latin at twelve, Greek at fourteen, and English at sixteen. He speaks English quite well for one who has never been in an English-speaking country before. When he goes back, he says he will have to serve in the German Army for one year. Everyone has to do it there. He says he can read Latin just as well as he can read English. I doubt if our boys could do as well.

This country was once the home of the buffaloes, but now not one is to be seen and even their robes are very scarce. In about an hour we shall be in Wyoming. Nebraska was formerly a great cattle country, but the great ranches are now being cut up into farms. Your father came very near settling here as teacher of History of Political Sciences at Lincoln (Nebraska University). This was in 1877. Instead of which he went with Ginn & Company. He thought he might teach here for a few years and then practice law and grow up with the state. I enclose in this a map showing you our route and where we enter the Yellowstone Park. I am enjoying it very much.

Your affectionate father,
Geo. A. Plimpton

June 22, 1910

My dear Francis:

Here I am in Idaho and on each side of the cars are large mountains and nothing but sage bush, no trees, and a little, very little grass. Now and then we see cows, sheep, and horses. A few moments ago we passed a flock of two thousand sheep. They say that back over the mountains there are plenty of sheep. Judging from the large quantity of bags of wool, there must be. We passed an extinct volcano; the crater was distinct and the whole region was lava. We are now where one river flows into the Gulf of California and the other river into the Columbia, and a short distance from here another river flows into the Gulf of Mexico. You would not think this country could support life, yet here and there by irrigation they manage to get good crops. These mountains are covered with snow and they say it will last until August.

Last night we arrived at Cheyenne, the capital of Wyoming. We waited there half an hour in order that our party might see the scenery by automobile. We were later out at the military post where four thousand soldiers live. The buildings are very fine. They have them there in case of emergency. Originally it was for the protection of the people against the Indians. At the present time there are one thousand negroes making a full regiment there. They say they make fine soldiers.

At Pocatello we saw quite a number of Indians; their reservation is nearby and our train passed it. We stopped and got some pictures. The Indians don't like to have their pictures taken but when I gave one twenty cents, he changed his mind.

The country around here is now being irrigated and land sells from $100 to $150 an acre. We see big wagons in which people live until they get their houses built. In a short time the whole valley will be full of people. They get the water from Snake River. Give me Lewis Farm. They say the people are mostly Mormons from Utah who have settled this valley. They used to believe in having several wives but this has been given up. The laws of the church and the United States are against it.

We arrived at Yellowstone Station at about 8:00 P.M. and after a good long walk went to a dance where the men paid ten cents for one dance or four dances for twenty-five cents. The music was from the gramophone.

We start at 7:45 for five days in the Yellowstone Park. I enclose the map. With love to all I am,

Your affectionate father,
Geo. A. Plimpton

Schiff Special Train
Pendleton, Oregon
June 27, 1910

My dear Francis:

I think I last wrote you at the Canyon Hotel. It is located near the great canyons through which the Yellowstone River flows. There are two great faces; one is 112 feet and the other is 360 feet. The sides of the canyon are in all sorts of colors so that they are very beautiful. The depth of their canyons is about twelve hundred feet. We saw three eagle nests and little eagles in each nest. They were on crags of rocks where no one could possibly get to them.

The morning I left Canyon Hotel I saw out of my window seven big black bears and three brown or cinnamon bears. As we drove along we saw a cow elk with her baby elk. We took lunch yesterday at Morris Geyser Basin, as they call it. Here all sorts of geysers—one they call the Minute because it plays every minute or less. Here is the plan of a geyser. There is a hole under a lake where the water flows down and flows over hot lava. When the water comes in contact with the lava it soon becomes boiling and then into steam and the result of this steam is that all the water is thrown out through another hole, which becomes the geyser. By the books and pictures I have sent you I guess you will get an idea of them.

We got to Ontario last night, Sunday. It seemed like getting home for I found everything in my stateroom in fine shape and two letters, one from Mr. Parkhurst. I wished that there was one from you but I guess I shall find it at Seattle Tuesday morning.

A short time ago we passed an Indian reservation, and again a little later when the Indians were getting ready to have a picnic, we should say. There were about thirty tents pitched or being pitched. There must have been several hundred Indians either there or on the way. I think I got a good picture of an Indian man on horseback. When I got his picture another Indian came up on horseback and said we must not take pictures unless I would pay for them, but while he was talking I got his picture. I hope that they will be good. Once a few of these Indians gathered here for their POW-WOW. Have had a fine time and I should have a great deal to tell you when I see you about this wonderful country, but I think I much prefer Lewis Farm to it. A great deal of attention is paid to Mr. Schiff and everybody is doing all they can for us.

Take good care of Grandmother and remember me to Hester and all the others.

Affectionately your father,
Geo. A. Plimpton

New Washington Hotel
Seattle, Washington
June 28, 1910

My dear Francis,

I wish I could tell you how pleased I was to get your letter this morning. It did me a lot of good and I showed it to Mr. Schiff and the rest of the party. I arrived here this morning at 8:00 and I am now thirty-five hundred miles from New York, as far if not further than if I were in London or Paris. On Thursday morning we go on board the *Ramona,* the boat that Mr. Schiff has engaged to take us to Alaska. The trip down the Columbia River was very interesting. High mountains on each side, and in two instances a large waterfall called the "Bridal Veil." In the river we saw a boat with a water wheel, as it looked to me, and they told me it was a wheel to catch fish. The fish, thinking it was a rapid, swam to get into it and then would be thrown into a box. This is a new way to me of fishing. It is sort of automatic. Before we got to the Columbia River we passed what is called the desert, one hundred miles long. Nothing grows except the sage bush, and the dust was fearful. It blows up from the river and is so bad at times that it stops the trains. It was blowing very hard yesterday and we were all covered with the sand. They put up boards just as we do to keep the snow from the tracks. I told them about the work Professor Saunders of Oltaires was doing in making trees grow in Outer Island. He has given a great deal of time and study to this question. They had never heard of him.

This city is not quite twenty-five years old and has, they say, 250,000 people. One would think that one was in New York. This hotel is a very fine one. They are moving a big hill near this hotel by washing it into the sea. The harbor is so deep—six hundred feet—that they would be glad that it filled up some. It is better for the ships, if they want to anchor. After you have read this letter you had better send it to Grandmother to read and tell her to keep it for you. Remember me to Mr. and Mrs. Lanier. I will let you know where to write me. Thank you very much for this fine letter.

Your affectionate father,
Geo. A. Plimpton

Steamer *Selkirk* on the Yukon River
Yukon Territory, Canada
July 13, 1910

My dear Francis:

Fifty-five years ago today your father was born in the old house at Plimptonville.... A good many things have happened since July 13, 1855. I wonder whether you will see as much progress from December 7, 1900, to December 7, 1955, as has occurred during my life. It does not seem possible for you to witness as much as I have. Electricity, the telegraph, telephone, electric light, wireless telegraphy, and all the mechanical inventions. It would seem as though there was little more to be done along these lines, and yet I imagine that this was the way my ancestors talked. I think the progress you will witness is the social improvement of people, especially the poor. You will see better government, more rational living, education, cost of living reduced, settlement of all disputes by arbitrators, and the abolition of wars. All nations are better acquainted with each other. International barriers are being broken down by means of commerce. The people whose guest I am on this trip are Jews, Mr. and Mrs. Jacob H. Schiff, and he said that today is his brother's birthday who lives in Frankfort, Germany. They celebrate the birthdays of all their relations and make a great point of it. Scarcely a day goes by when they don't send a telegram to one of their relations in this country or in Europe congratulating them and giving them their best wishes. The devotion of the Jews to their own family and to their own race is beautiful. They believe, as my mother taught us, that we must work for the family, help your brother and sister all that you can. Their advancement is for advantages in every way.

It is taking us five days to make the trip from Dawson to White Horse. It took us two-and-a-half days going from White Horse to Dawson. We are pushing a large barge in front of us and it gives us a good chance to walk and exercise, as it happens to be empty. Every twenty-five miles or more we stop and take in wood. This is piled up on the banks of the river and is wood for making steam. I got out the other day to exercise by helping them load. The exercise did me a lot of good. One must do a lot of walking and eat very little.

Captain Jarvis is a very interesting man. He was in the revenue service of the United States until five years ago. He was captain of a government vessel, *Bear*, that went to the Arctic Ocean and along the coast of Alaska and saw that the people obeyed the laws of the United States in regard to sealing, fishing, etc.

> Your affectionate father,
> Geo. A. Plimpton
> S. S. *Ramona*

102

White Horse, Yukon Territory, Canada
July 18, 1910

My dear Francis,

. . .While we were here we took this big stage with four horses and went to the Atlas Copper Mines about six miles from here. Here we were received by Mr. Greenough, the owner, and he showed us the copper ore. He says that he has in sight a million tons of it, and that the copper ore averages three-and-a-half percent. That is, of one hundred pounds, three-and-a-half pounds would be copper. In this copper ore there is some good silver and more iron. The ore is shipped to Tacoma, Washington, where it is smelted—that is, the iron, silver, and copper are separated. He has built a big house where the men all live and has a big gramophone to entertain them. He paid $500,000 for the mine and thinks he will make $1.85 for every ton of ore he ships to Tacoma. I got some specimens to show you.

A short distance from White Horse are the rapids. . . there are very high bluffs on each side of it and the water runs very swiftly.

I had a chance to pick up some gold nuggets; a miner brought them in to town to sell. He told me he and two other men brought in four thousand dollars in gold dust as the result of a year's work. His mine was 150 miles from here. I met another miner who came from Boston. He was going to walk to his mine, which he said was two hundred miles away. He said when he was in Boston that he saw a house in Winthrop, Massachusetts. A lady, who had some diamonds in the house, offered him a certain amount if he would recover them. He spent four days and got five hundred dollars for finding them. Said his knowledge of mining helped him out. I saw an interesting log cabin and asked the man if I could look in, and he said yes. He showed me his refrigerator, which consisted of a dumbwaiter down in the ground. As the ground is frozen all the time, all you have to do is dig a hole and put your food there and it will keep. There were a dozen cabins like his and all occupied by single men. They do their own cooking, washing, mending, etc., but they stay only about six months, although some stay the whole year.

   . . . My dear boy, I am your affectionate father.

Geo. A. Plimpton

Off Cape St. Elias, Pacific Ocean
July 24, 1910

My dear Francis,

    It is Sunday and there is no church to attend, but when one sees this great ocean, the great mountains at a distance covered with snow, the beautiful sky, one can't help thinking of one's creator and how thankful we all ought to be that we live in this beautiful and wonderful world. I think I have realized as never before what a beautiful world we have. The point of view one has in life makes all the difference in the world with one as to happiness. Some think of life as only what they can get out of it, those things that they can eat, drink, wear, or that appeal to their passion or pleasure. They think only of themselves and care nothing about neighbors or other people. These wonders appeal only to them as they minister to their needs. You and I have been brought up to believe that we are here to work not for ourselves but for others; as the Bible says, he "that loseth himself shall find himself." The boy who is forever thinking of himself and not of other boys is a selfish boy and sooner or later he finds that no boy wants to be with him, and just the opposite occurs when the boy cares for someone besides himself. . . .

Your affectionate father,
Geo. A. Plimpton